THE FAMILY
HANDYMAN
DO-IT-YOURSELF
ENCYCLOPEDIA

THE FAMILY
HANDYMAN

DO-IT-YOURSELF

ENCYCLOPEDIA

*Comprehensive How-To-Series
for the entire family...
containing material from
The Illustrated
Do-It-Yourself Encyclopedia
...written in simple language with
full step-by-step instructions
and profusely illustrated*

Illustrated Edition

VOLUME
6
Fir-Fur

Published by arrangement with
Universal Publishing & Distributing
Corporation, Publisher of The
Family Handyman magazine.

ACKNOWLEDGMENTS

The editors of this series would like to express their thanks and appreciation to the following companies for their assistance in preparing special sections within this volume, for their technical advice and their permission to use special material, photographs, art and educational charts.

ARMSTRONG CORK CO. • E. L. BRUCE CO. • FORMICA CO. • JOHNS-MANVILLE CO. • ALLEN LARKIN ASSOCIATES • MARSH WALL PRODUCTS, INC. • MASTIC TILE COMPANY • MODERNFOLD DOORS • MONSANTO CHEMICAL CO. • MOSAIC TILE CO. • NATURAL RUBBER BUREAU • PIERCE & STEVENS, INC. • PORTLAND CEMENT ASSOCIATION • RED DEVIL TOOLS, INC. • RUBBER MANUFACTURERS ASSOCIATION • THE STANLEY WORKS • SUPERIOR FIREPLACE CO. • TIMBER ENGINEERING CO. • UNIVERSITY SPEAKERS, INC. • VEGA INDUSTRIES, INC.

For their combined efforts in revising this work, the Publishers wish to thank Morton Waters, Editorial Director of THE FAMILY HANDYMAN Magazine, and Patrick O'Rourke, of Morpad, Inc., Graphic Designers.

Fire Wall

A fire-resistant transverse bulkhead to set the engine apart from the rest of the automobile. The wall directly below and behind the dashboard in a car is a fire wall to protect the rest of the car if a fire breaks out in the engine.

Within the home, a fire wall serves the same purpose—to retard the spreading of a fire. It is made of an incombustible material—Sheet-rock, brick or concrete—and is used:

(a) when the garage is part of the house, to provide a fire-resistant wall between the garage and house; and

(b) when a basement is finished, to set the section around the furnace off from the rest of the basement.

Firebrick

This is a special type of brick which is capable of withstanding the effects of great heat. It is used to line the inside of a furnace and often used to line the inside of a barbecue built outdoors.

Fireplaces

A fireplace is ordinarily considered appropriate to a living room, dining room, and bedroom; however, basement and porch fireplaces are gaining in favor with the householder.

All fireplaces should be built in accordance with a few simple essentials of correct design if satisfactory performance is to be real-

Prefabricated fireplace is easily added in any room of the house and can be installed with a few hand tools. It comes with its own chimney, thereby eliminating expensive masonry work.

Photograph courtesy of Uni-Bilt Division, Vega Industries, Inc.

This fireplace is covered with a plastic finished hardboard in a woodgrain pattern, which is also used as a wainscot around the rest of the room.

Photograph courtesy of Marsh Wall Products, Inc.

ized. They should be of a size best suited to the room in which they are to be used from the standpoint of appearance and operation. If too small, they may function properly but do not throw out sufficient heat. If they are too large, a fire that would fill the combustion chamber would be entirely too hot for the room and would waste fuel.

The location of the chimney, which determines the location of the fireplace, is too often governed by structural considerations only. A fireplace suggests a fireside group and a reasonable degree of seclusion and therefore, especially in the living room, it should not be near doors to passageways of the house.

Characteristics

The principal warming effect of a fireplace is produced by the radi-

ant heat from the fire and from the hot back, sides, and hearth. In the ordinary fireplace practically no heating effect is produced by convection, that is, by air current. Air passes through the fire and up the chimney, carrying with it the heat absorbed from the fire; at the same time outside air of a lower temperature is drawn into the room. The effect of the cold air thus brought into the room is particularly noticeable farthest from the fire.

Modified Fireplaces

The Franklin stove is a type of modified fireplace. There are also modified fireplaces manufactured as units of heavy metal, designed to be set into place and concealed by the usual brickwork or other construction, so that no practical change in mantel design is required by their use. The modifications are built-in standard parts of the fireplace—only the grilles show.

One advantage claimed for modified fireplace units is that the correctly designed and proportioned firebox, manufactured with throat, damper, smoke shelf, and chamber, provides a form for the masonry, thus reducing the risk of failure and assuring a smokeless fireplace. However, there is no excuse for using incorrect proportions; and the desirability of using a foolproof form, as provided by the modified unit, merely to obtain good proportions should be considered from the standpoint of cost. Even though the unit is well designed, it will not operate properly if the chimney is inadequate; therefore, the rules for correct chimney construction must be adhered to with the modified unit as well as with the ordinary fireplace.

Manufacturers claim labor and materials saved tend to offset the purchase price of the unit; also that the saving in fuel justifies any net increase in first cost. A minimum life of 20 years is claimed for the type and thickness of metal commonly used today in these units.

Field tests have proved that, when properly installed, the better designs of modified-fireplace units circulate heat into the cold corners of rooms and will deliver heated air through

This simple fireplace has ceramic tiles around the fireplace opening. Many varieties of these tiles are available.

Photograph courtesy of The Mosaic Tile Co.

Inviting and warm, a fireplace and wood mantel add to this decorating scheme.
Photograph courtesy of Superior Fireplace Co.

ducts to adjoining or upper rooms. For example, heat could be diverted to a bathroom from a living-room fireplace.

The quantity and temperature of the heated air discharged from the grilles were measured to determine the merits of the convection features. These measurements showed that very appreciable amounts of convected heat are produced by the modified unit when properly installed and operated. Discharge-air temperatures in excess of 200°F were attained from some of the units tested. The heated air delivered from the discharge grilles of some of the medium-sized units represented a heating effect equivalent to that from nearly 40 square feet of cast-iron radiation of the ordinary hot-water heating system, or sufficient to heat a 15′ by 18′ room built with average tightness to 70°F when the outside temperature is 40°F. Additional convected heat can be produced with some models by the use of forced-circulation fans.

However, the nature of operation, with the unavoidably large quantity of heated air passing up the stack, makes the inherent over-all efficiency of any fireplace relatively low. Therefore, claims for an increased efficiency of modified fireplaces should be understood merely as constituting an improvement over the ordinary fireplace and not over stoves or central heating plants.

Selecting a Fireplace

When a fireplace is being selected the kind of fuel to be burned should be considered; also, the design should harmonize with the room in proportion and detail.

In Colonial days, when cordwood was plentiful, fireplaces 7′ wide and 5′ high were common, especially used in kitchens for cooking. They required large amounts of fuel and too frequently were smokey.

Where cordwood (4′ long) is cut in half, a 30″ width is desirable for a fireplace; but, where coal is burned, the opening can be narrower. Thirty inches is a practical height for the convenient tending of a fire where the width is less than 6′; openings about 30″ wide are generally made with square corners. The higher the opening, the greater the chance of a smokey fireplace.

In general, the wider the opening, the greater should be the depth.

A shallow opening throws out relatively more heat than a deep one of the same width but accommodates smaller pieces of wood; thus it becomes a question of preference between a greater depth which permits the use of large logs that burn longer and a shallower depth which takes smaller-sized wood but throws out more heat.

In small fireplaces a depth of 12″ will permit good draft if the throat is constructed as explained above, but a minimum depth of 16″ to 18″ is advised to lessen the danger of brands falling out on floor.

As a rule, fireplaces on the second floor are smaller than those on the first floor and it is well to follow this practice because the flue height is less for second-floor fireplaces.

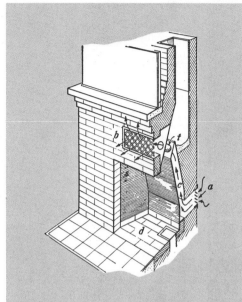

In this modified fireplace air enters the inlet, a, from outside and is heated as it rises by natural circulation through the back chamber, c, and the tubes, t, being discharged into the room from the register, b. Air for supporting combustion is drawn into the fire at d and passes between the tubes up the flue. A damper is also provided to close the air inlet.

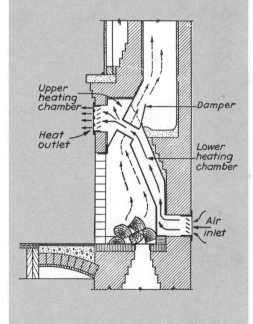

should be increased for larger rooms, but all other dimensions should be taken from the table "Recommended Dimensions for Fireplaces."

Units providing for burning gas are often built in to resemble fireplaces.

Pleasing designs result from exercising good taste in use of materials and mantels that suit the room. The essentials for safety and utility, however, should not be sacrificed for style.

Construction

The ordinary fireplace is constructed generally with these essentials: (1) that the flue have the proper area, (2) that the throat be correctly constructed and have suitable damper, (3) that the chimney be high enough for a good draft, (4) that the shape of the fireplace be such as to direct a maximum amount of radiated heat into the room, and (5) that a properly constructed smoke chamber be provided.

Dimensions

The table, "Recommended Dimensions for Fireplaces," gives recommended dimensions for fireplaces of various widths and heights.

If a damper is installed, the width of the opening will depend on the width of the damper frame, the size of which is fixed by the width and depth of the fireplace and the slope of the back wall.

The width of the throat proper is determined by the opening of hinged damper cover. The full damper opening should never be less than the flue area. Responsible manufacturers of fireplace equipment give valuable

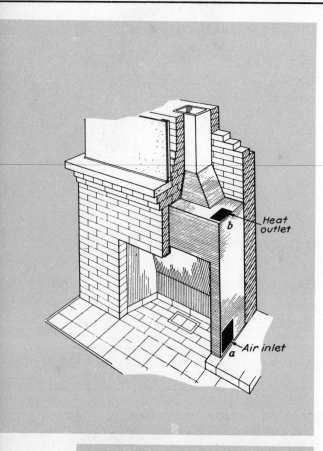

In this fireplace the air is not drawn in directly from outdoors but through the inlet by contact with the metal sides and back of the fireplace, rises by natural circulation, and is discharged back into the room from the outlet, b, or to another room on the same floor or in the second story. The inlets and outlets are connected to registers which may be located at the front of the fireplace. The registers may be located on the ends of the fireplace or on the wall of an adjacent room.

Unless a fireplace 6' wide is fully 28" deep, the logs will have to be split, and some advantage of the wide opening will be lost.

Screens of suitable design should be placed in front of all fireplaces.

A fireplace 30" to 36" wide is generally suitable for a room having 300 square feet of floor. The width

assistance in the selection of a suitable damper for a given fireplace. A well-designed and well-installed damper should be regarded as essential in cold climates.

When no damper is used, the throat opening should be 4 inches for fireplaces not exceeding 4 feet in height.

Prefabricated Fireplace

To fill the need for a low-cost fireplace that eliminates expensive masonry construction, a completely prefabricated fireplace and chimney have been developed. The unit, complete with chimney, can be installed in four to six manhours, according to the manufacturer who developed the Uni-Bilt.

This ready-made fireplace, which meets Underwriters' Laboratory requirements, can be mounted flush with the wall or recessed into it. The cantilever designed hearth, which is 15" above the floor, burns wood up to 27" long. The outer shell of the fireplace is steel with stainless steel trim. The firebox itself is formed of high-impact ceramic material.

Except for the trim, the complete unit is prime coated and ready to paint with any interior paint to harmonize with the room decorating scheme. A flexible hearth screen comes with the fireplace to prevent sparks from flying out of the fireplace into the room.

Preformed Firebox

Fireplace construction is an exacting art. While some handymen would like to build a fireplace from scratch, others undoubtedly will be content to install a prefabricated fireplace and chimney while others would like to eliminate the compli-

A shallow fireplace, with a copper hood, throws out considerable heat after the hood gets hot. The wall should be of fire-resistant masonry.

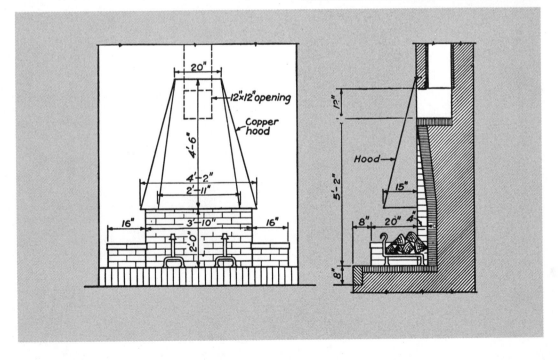

cated firebox construction and do the rest of the work themselves. A preformed metal unit, Heatform, will enable the handyman to eliminate the complicated planning and building of the firebox.

The units are available in different styles so that you can build any type of fireplace—Colonial to Contemporary—around the basic frame. Heatform is a double-walled metal unit consisting of a firebox, throat, dome and heat control damper. It forms a guide around which masonry walls of the fireplace can be built easily and economically.

For those who wish to build a complete unit themselves, there are full details in the remainder of this section.

Hearth

The hearth in conventional fireplaces should be about flush with the floor, for sweepings may then be brushed into the fireplace. When there is a basement, an ash dump located in the hearth near the back of the fireplace is convenient. The dump consists of a metal frame about 5″ by 8″ with a plate, generally pivoted, through which ashes can be dropped into a pit below.

In buildings with wooden floors the hearth in front of the fireplace should be supported by masonry trimmer arches or other fire-resistant construction. Hearths should project at least 16″ from the chimney breast and should be of brick, stone, terra cotta, or reinforced concrete not less

Recommended Dimensions for Fireplaces

Opening Width Inches	Opening Height Inches	Depth Inches	Minimum back (horizontal) Inches	Vertical back wall Inches	Inclined back wall Inches	Outside dimensions of standard rectangular flue lining Inches	Inside diameter of standard round flue lining Inches
24	24	16–18	14	14	16	8½ x 8½	10
28	24	16–18	14	14	16	8½ x 8½	10
24	28	16–18	14	14	20	8½ x 8½	10
30	28	16–18	16	14	20	8½ x 13	10
36	28	16–18	22	14	20	8½ x 13	12
42	28	16–18	28	14	20	8½ x 18	12
36	32	18–20	20	14	24	8½ x 18	12
42	32	18–20	26	14	24	13 x 13	12
48	32	18–20	32	14	24	13 x 13	15
42	36	18–20	26	14	28	13 x 13	15
48	36	18–20	32	14	28	13 x 18	15
54	36	18–20	38	14	28	13 x 18	15
60	36	18–20	44	14	28	13 x 18	15
42	40	20–22	24	17	29	13 x 13	15
48	40	20–22	30	17	29	13 x 18	15
54	40	20–22	36	17	29	13 x 18	15
60	40	20–22	42	17	29	18 x 18	18
66	40	20–22	48	17	29	18 x 18	18
72	40	22–28	51	17	29	18 x 18	18

than 4″ thick. The length of the hearth should be not less than the width of the fireplace opening plus 16″. Wooden centering under trimmer arches may be removed after the mortar has set, though it is more frequently left in pace.

Wall Thickness

The walls of fireplaces should never be less than 8″ thick, and if of stone they should be at least 12″ thick. When built of stone or hard-burned brick, the back and sides are often not lined with firebrick, but it is better to use firebrick laid in fire clay. When firebricks are laid flat with the long edges exposed there is less danger of their falling out. They are generally placed on edge, however, forming a 2″ protection, in which case metal ties should be built into the main brickwork to hold the 2″ firebrick veneer in place. Thick metal backs and sides are sometimes used as lining. When a grate for burning coal or coke is built in, firebrick at least 2″ thick should be added to the fireplace back unless the grate has a solid iron back and is only set in with an air space behind it.

Jambs

The jambs should be wide enough to give stability and a pleasing appearance; they are frequently faced with ornamental brick or tile. For an opening 3″ wide or less, a 12″ or 16″ width is generally sufficient, depending on whether a wood mantel is used or the jambs are of exposed masonry. The edges of a wood mantel should be kept at least 8″

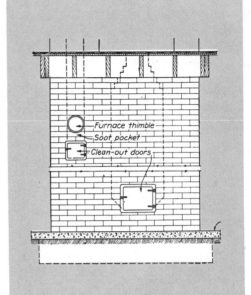

The ashpit should be of tight masonry and should be provided with a tightly fitting iron clean-out door and frame about 10″ by 12″. A clean-out for the furnace flue as shown is sometimes provided.

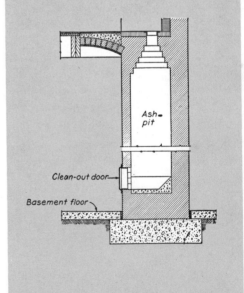

from the fireplace opening. For wider openings and large rooms, similar proportions should be kept.

Lintel

Lintels of ½"x3" bars, 3½"x 3½"x¼" angle irons, or damper frames are used to support the masonry over the opening or ordinary fireplaces. Heavier lintel irons are required for wider openings.

Where a masonry arch is used over the opening, the jambs should be heavy enough to resist the thrust of the arch. Arches over openings less than 4' wide seldom sag, but sagging is not uncommon in wider fireplaces, especially where massive masonry is used.

Throat

The sides of the fireplace should be vertical up to the throat, or damper opening. The throat should be 6" to 8" or more above the bottom of the lintel and have an area not less than that of the flue and a length equal to the width of the fireplace opening. Starting 5" above the throat, the sides should be drawn in to equal the flue area.

Proper throat construction is necessary to a successful fireplace and the builder must make certain that the side walls are carried up perpendicularly until the throat is passed and that the full length of opening is provided.

Smoke Shelf and Chamber

The smoke shelf is made by setting the brickwork back at the top of the throat to the line of the flue

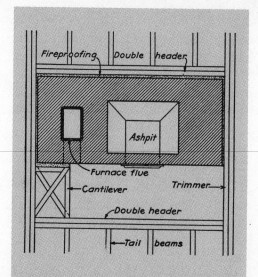

Where a header is more than 4' in length, it should be doubled, as shown. Headers supporting more than four tail beams should have ends supported in metal joist hangers. The framing may be placed ½" from the chimney because the masonry is 8" thick.

wall for the full length of the throat. Its depth may vary from 6" to 12" or more, depending on the depth of the fireplace.

The smoke chamber is the space extending from the top of the throat up to the bottom of the flue proper and between the side walls. The walls should be drawn inward 30° to the vertical after the top of the throat is passed and smoothly plastered with cement mortar not less than ½" thick.

Damper

A properly designed damper affords a means of regulating the draft and prevents excessive loss of heat from the room when the fire is out. A damper consists of a cast-iron frame with a lid hinged so that the width of the throat opening may be

Notice the beautiful pattern and texture of the stone work in this Model "A" Heatform fireplace, and note too that the stones have been spaced for inlets and outlets. This is recommended provided sufficient open space is left for the free flow of air. Here, also, the owner has used antique accessories with modern design.

Photograph courtesy of Superior Fireplace Co.

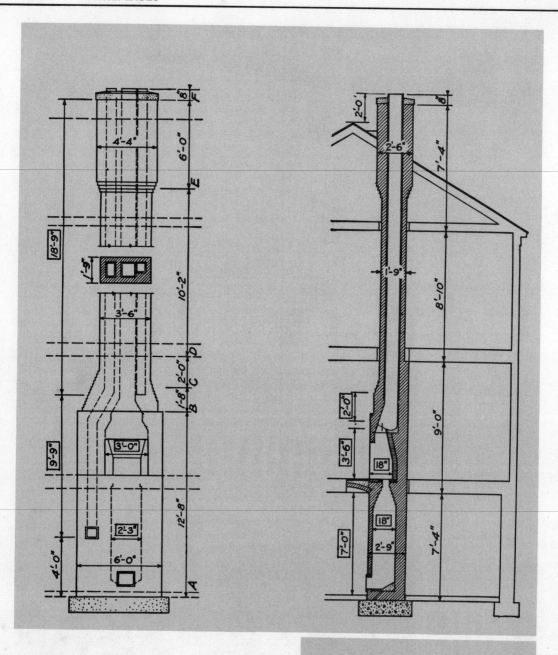

varied from a closed to a wide-open position. Various patterns are on the market, some designed to support the masonry over the opening, others requiring lintel irons.

A roaring pine fire may require a full-throat opening, but slow-burning hardwood logs may need only 1″ or 2″ of opening. Regulating the open-

Diagram showing front view and cross section of an entire chimney such as is commonly built to serve a furnace, fireplace, and kitchen stove. Two sets of dimensions are given; those in rectangles refer to the approximate sizes of the voids or openings, the others refer to the outside dimensions of the brickwork. These are used in estimating the quantities of brick required.

ing according to the kind of fire prevents waste of heat up the chimney. Closing the damper in summer keeps flies, mosquitos, and other insects from entering the house down the chimney.

In houses heated by furnaces or other modern systems, lack of a damper in the fireplace flue may interfere with uniform heating, particularly in very cold windy weather, whether or not there is a fire on the hearth. When air heated by the furnace is carried up the chimney there is a waste of the furnace fuel, but a damper partially open serves a slow fire of hardwood without smoking the room or wasting heated air from the main heating system.

Flue

The area of lined flues should be a twelfth or more of the fireplace opening, provided the chimney is at least 22′ in height, measured from the hearth. If the flue is shorter than 22′ or if it is unlined, its area should be made a tenth or more of the fireplace opening. A fireplace which, for instance, has an opening of 7.5 square feet, or approximately 1,080 square inches, needs a flue area of approximately 90 square inches; a rectangular flue, 8½″x18″, outside dimensions, or a round flue with a 12″ inside diameter might be used, as these are the nearest commercial sizes of lining. It is seldom possible to obtain lining having exactly the required area, but the inside area should never be less than that prescribed above. A 13″x13″ flue was selected for convenience when combining with the other flues. If the flue is built of brick and is unlined,

Sizes of Fireplace Flue Linings[1]		
Area of fireplace opening	Outside dimensions of standard rectangular flue lining	Inside diameter of standard round flue lining
Square inches	Inches	Inches
600	8½ x 8½	10
800	8½ x 13	10
1,000	8½ x 18	12
1,200	8½ x 18	12
1,400	13 x 13	12
1,600	13 x 13	15
1,800	13 x 18	15
2,000	13 x 18	15
2,200	13 x 18	15
2,400	18 x 18	18
2,600	18 x 18	18
2,800	18 x 18	18
3,000	18 x 18	18

[1]Based on a flue area equal to one-twelfth the fireplace opening.

its area should be approximately one-tenth of the fireplace opening, or 108 square inches. It would probably be made 8″x16″ (128 square inches) because brickwork can be laid to better advantage when the dimensions of the flue are multiples of 4″.

The Table, "Sizes of Fireplace Flue Linings," is convenient in selecting the proper size of flue or for determining the size of fireplace opening for an existing flue. The area of the fireplace opening in square inches is obtained by multiplying the width by the height, both measured in inches.

Refer to *CHIMNEY CONSTRUCTION.*

Also *CHIMNEY REPAIRS.*

This common red brick fireplace is built around the Model "A" Heatform. Split bricks have been spaced for the inlet and outlet grilles to allow maximum warm air passage.

Smoky Fireplace

When a fireplace smokes, it should be examined to make certain that the essential requirements of construction have been fulfilled. If the chimney is not stopped up with fallen brick and the mortar joints are not loose, note whether nearby trees or tall structures cause eddies down the flue. To determine whether the fireplace opening is in correct proportion to the flue area, hold a piece of sheet metal across the top face of the fireplace opening and then gradually lower it, making the opening smaller until smoke does not come into the room. Mark at the lower edge of the metal on the sides of the fireplace. The opening may then be reduced by building in a metal shield or hood across the top so that its lower edge is at the marks made during the test. The trouble can generally be remedied in another way by increasing the height of the flue.

Soot Removal

Refer to the section on *CHIMNEY REPAIRS*.

Cleaning Brickwork

When the brickwork around the fireplace becomes soiled, it may be scrubbed with a brush dipped into a solution of 1 tablespoonful of trisodium phosphate to a gallon of water. Rinse off with clear water, and then dry with a cloth.

But if the bricks are stained, they may need to be bleached. For this

Colorful flagstone adds to the appearance of this fireplace. Both the cool air inlets and warm air outlets of the preformed fireplace unit have been located on the return sides of the fireplace.

An attractive brick fireplace. Note the cool air inlets and warm outlets are formed right into the masonry of the fireplace.

Photographs courtesy of Superior Fireplace Co.

purpose use about 1¼ lbs. of oxalic acid crystals in a gallon of warm water, adding sufficient lime or whiting to form a soft paste. (Caution: oxalic acid is a poison, and it must be handled carefully!) Use a broad knife or spatula to spread this paste over the stained parts of the brickwork. Let it remain about 15 minutes, then scrape off the paste. Wash the bricks with clear water, then dry with a cloth.

Should the cleaning or bleaching not remove the dirt or stains from the bricks, try putting a thin oil stain over them, choosing the same or perhaps a little darker color than the bricks. This will give them a uniform dark appearance.

Hearth Tiles

To keep the hearth looking its best, wash the tiles with warm, soapy water, then rinse with clear water. When completely dry, rub a coat of wax over them. This not only adds to their good appearance but makes the tiles more dirt-resistant.

When Fireplace is Unused

During the warm months when the fireplace is left unlighted, instead of the open, gaping space you may want to camouflage it in a decorative manner. Here are some suggestions: Build a wood trellis to stand in front of the fireplace; place two or three small potted foliage plants in front of the trellis and train the leaves over it. Or, without the trellis, place three or four large pots of upright foliage plants in front of the fireplace; these will cover the open space. (Refer to the section of *PLANTS FOR THE HOME* for a choice of foliage plants.) Or you may use a small decorative straight or folding screen in front of the unused fireplace.

Cement blocks were used as a building medium in this modern fireplace built around a 38 Model "S" Heatform. The raised hearth provides informal seating capacity, as well as a permanent place for the television. The designer preferred to form the cool air inlet and warm air outlet of the masonry used in the fireplace and wall. Good judgment was exercised in placing the cool air inlet at floor level, which assures a greater volume of warm air circulation and warmer floors.

Photograph courtesy of Superior Fireplace Co.

Fireplace, Outdoors

See *BARBECUE*.

Fishtape

Fishtape or an electrical snake is used to fish wires through a wall, floor, pipe or conduit. It is light and flexible, but must be strong. When purchasing fishtape in a hardware store, get a 50′ or 100′ roll.

When using fishtape, lubricate it with soapstone or talcum powder to make it easier to handle. The end of the tape is shaped into a hook and the wires attached to it.

To fish a wire cable through a wall, floor, pipe or conduit, push the wire completely through and connect the cable to the hook at one end. Then slowly pull the cable through by pulling on the tape. It is important to form a perfect knot with the cable or else it will come loose as it is fished through.

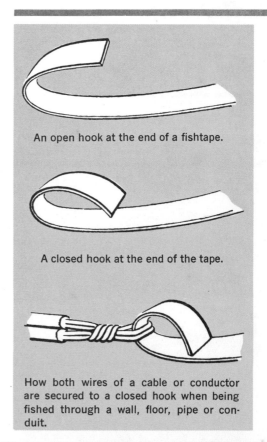

An open hook at the end of a fishtape.

A closed hook at the end of the tape.

How both wires of a cable or conductor are secured to a closed hook when being fished through a wall, floor, pipe or conduit.

Fixture Splice

A special type of joining between the main electric wires and the wires from the electrical ceiling or wall fixture. Frequently, the main electric wire is solid whereas the fixture wire is stranded.

Both can be joined with a solderless connector. However, many handymen prefer to twist the wires together, solder and then tape them. Here's how to make a fixture splice:

1. After removing the insulation

from both wires, make certain that the wires are clean.

2. Twist the stranded wire of the fixture tightly around the solid wire of the main electrical line.

3. Then bend the solid wire over with a pliers to hold the two together firmly.

4. Heat the wires and solder them.

5. Cover the splice with rubber tape followed by friction tape, or use plastic tape.

Also see *ELECTRICAL WIRING*.

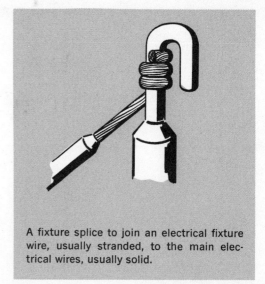

A fixture splice to join an electrical fixture wire, usually stranded, to the main electrical wires, usually solid.

Flagstone

Flagstone can be used to make a decorative patio and garden walk. Here the flagstones are combined with brick to make an outdoor living and play area.

Flagstone and slate are large slabs of limestone, shale or sandstone, which come in varying widths and lengths in thicknesses ranging from about ¾" to 2". Generally, they are irregular in shape although they can be bought cut and matched.

Available in a broad range of colors—red, pink, gray, buff, orange, slate and charcoal—these stones are used for patios, terraces, walks, exterior walls, occasionally floors, and around fireplaces.

Flagstones can be set on a concrete base or when used outdoors, set on gravel or sand. However, unless the flagstone is set on concrete, it should be at least 1½" thick to withstand wear and tear in normal use.

The handyman can cut the stone to size himself. A mason's hammer does an effective job, if you have one handy, or you can use a cold chisel and hammer, holding the flagstone over a solid base, such as a steel I-beam.

Also see *PATIOS*.

Flagstone can not only be set over concrete to make a decorative walk but are excellent for outdoor steps as well.

Cutting flagstone with a mason's hammer.

Flange

This is a flat rim on the end of an iron pipe fitting with holes in it to permit the bolting of the unit to a surface or another flange. It is often used when making handrails on stairways, or when making awning frames out of pipe.

Flange Nut

A flange nut.

A special nut with a flange as an integral part is called a flange nut. It is used instead of a separate washer and a nut. The flange end of the nut is set flush against the surface to be held.

Flaring Tool

Copper tubing joined with flared fittings requires a special tool to spread or flare the ends. The flaring tool comes in several forms. There are individual flaring rods made to fit specific size tubing, or adjustable flaring tools which can be used with several different sizes of tubing.

Also see *PLUMBING*.

An adjustable flaring tool is used to spread the end of different diameter copper tubing for use with flared fittings.

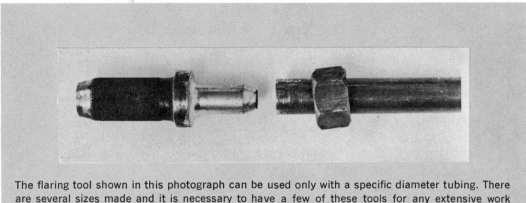

The flaring tool shown in this photograph can be used only with a specific diameter tubing. There are several sizes made and it is necessary to have a few of these tools for any extensive work with copper tubing.

Flash Point

This is the temperature at which an oil gives off vapor in sufficient quantity to ignite if a spark or flame is present. An open can of paint placed in the sun or next to heat is a fire hazard if the oil in the can reaches the flash-point level.

Flashing

By means of a lap joint, flashing may be used to make watertight the angle where a roof meets an intersecting surface. Flashing is installed at junctions between roof and walls, chimneys, skylights, and similar places, and in valleys or depressions where two planes of a roof join. Flashing around walls, chimneys, or other vertical surfaces is designed to shed water from the joint, causing it to seek lower levels; flashing in valleys is intended to conduct the water to the gutters. Corrosion-resistant flashing material should be used wherever possible.

For further information on flashing, see the section on *CHIMNEY CONSTRUCTION*, also section on *ROOF*.

Methods of Application

Several materials (cut in strips or pieces) such as tin or terneplate, galvanized iron, slate, sheet copper, soft lead sheets, sheet aluminum, or flashing felt are used for flashing. The methods of applying the different materials vary according to conditions, and recommendations by manufacturers of roofing materials should be followed if furnished.

There are several different methods of fastening the upper edge of flashing places against a vertical surface, depending upon the material in the vertical surface. When

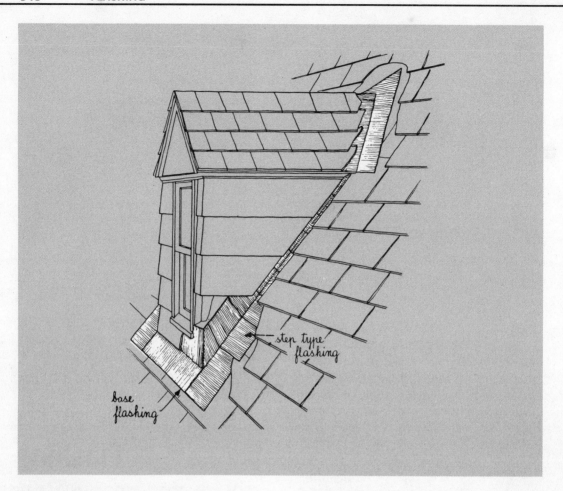

step type flashing

base flashing

placed against a brick or other masonry surface, the upper edge is usually bent and inserted into a groove or joint in the masonry, and the crack is sealed with flashing cement.

Sometimes two pieces of flashing are used in connection with masonry walls. The first is bent in the middle and the upper half is nailed to the vertical surface of the wall; the lower half is then nailed over one thickness of roofing and covered by another thickness. The second piece, known as counterflashing, is hung over the first to form an apron. It is suspended by bending the upper edge and inserting it into a joint in the vertical surface of the masonry. Since the two

pieces of flashing are independent of each other, they are not likely to break if parts of the building settle or shrink.

Against stucco or other plastered walls, the upper edge of the flashing may be inserted behind the lath or fastened in such a way that it will be covered by the plaster when it is applied. In frame construction, the upper edge of the flashing is generally run up behind the siding or shingles.

Where the vertical surface intersects another surface in a horizontal line, as at the face of a chimney near the eaves or at a horizontal roof line at the base of a wall, flashing is generally extended down over

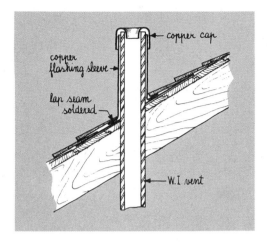

the top or next to the top course of roofing and nailed down after the space to be lapped has been coated with flashing cement to make a tight joint. Similarly, when a roof covered with roofing or other flat roofing material meets a vertical surface in a horizontal intersection, the flashing from the vertical surface usually extends down and is sealed and nailed on top of the roofing.

However, where a roof meets a vertical surface in a sloping line, such as along the sides of a chimney on a sloping roof, and the roofing consists of shingles or similarly lapped material, base and cap flashing are generally employed. The base and cap flashing means that, working up-

ward on the roof, each succeeding piece of flashing extends from the vertical surface down over a shingle on the roof and is then covered by the next higher shingle course. This course is then covered by the next higher piece of flashing and so on up the slope. For an intersection where roll roofing is used, it is either turned up under the side wall material or the flashing is nailed over it, with flashing cement between to seal the joint.

At the up-slope face of a chimney which protrudes through a sloping roof a so-called cricket or saddle is usually constructed in the roof's surface. As the name "saddle" indicates, it is a small ridge formed behind the chimney to divide the water running down the roof and throw it to each side away from the chimney instead of allowing it to dam up back of it. Water accumulating back of the chimney might eventually result in leakage at that point. The joint between the chimney and cricket is also flashed.

Both open and closed valleys are used in roof construction. In an open valley the flashing is applied before the roofing is laid. The roofing material is then extended over

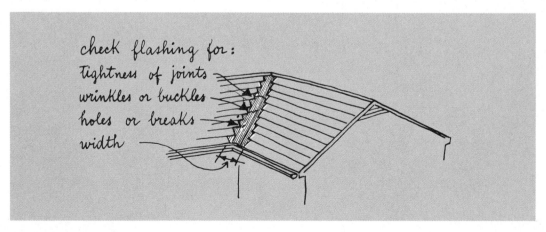

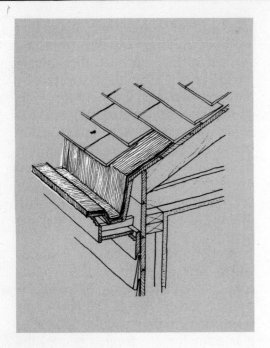

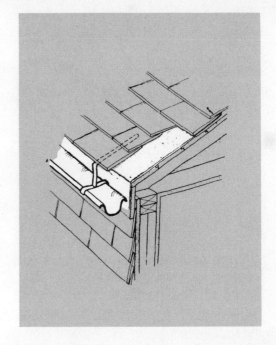

the flashing to make a lap joint. The center portion of the flashing is visible for the entire length and the open space is usually wider at the bottom than near the ridge to accommodate the increasing volume of water as it nears the eaves. In the closed valley, the flashing is inserted by the base and cap flashing method to make an unbroken surface which is generally considered more pleasing in appearance. The flashing material in either case should be wide enough to extend under the roofing material a sufficient distance to insure good protection.

Causes of Leakage

Occasionally metal wall flashing may warp and be drawn out of the groove or joint in the vertical surface or, when roll roofing is used, it may break at its junction with the vertical surface, allowing water to run down behind it. The force of the wind may tear flashing loose from the face of the roofing and water will enter during heavy rains. Valley flashings, if too narrow, may allow backed-up water to find its way under the roofing. This seeping sometimes occurs when the valleys are dammed up with snow and ice. Flashing material in valleys may corrode or break, causing cracks or holes through which water may enter and drip through the joint below.

To Make Repairs

The approximate location of leaks in flashing may often be determined by looking for wet spots on the walls or ceiling of the house. Carefully examine the flashing above and near such spots to ascertain the exact location and cause of leakage if possible. If the leak is near a chimney or below the junction between the roof and a vertical wall or similar surface, the flashing should be inspected to see whether it has become loosened. It

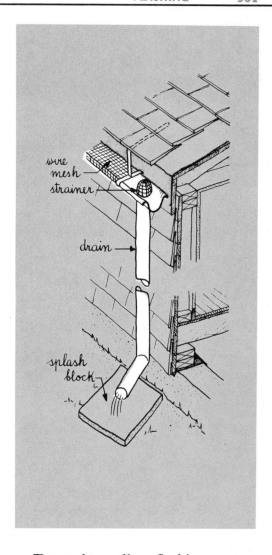

may be found that the flashing needs replacing or that the mortar has fallen out and needs repointing. Flashing cement and similar compounds are useful and effective in sealing cracks around flashing.

If the flashing that extends over the top of roofing—as the base of a vertical surface—becomes loosened, it should be nailed down after the underside of the lap has been well coated with flashing cement. The flashing cement serves to seal the spaces around nails and the cracks along the edges which otherwise might allow leakage. It is also best to use short nails in order to avoid penetration of roof boards.

When exposed metal flashing shows signs of rusting, it should be cleaned with a wire brush and painted with a good metal paint to preserve it from further corrosion. This paint coat should be examined at regular intervals and renewed when it shows signs of wear.

To make valley flashing water-tight, it is advisable to cover the portion to be overlapped with flashing cement immediately before applying the roof covering. This should seal the space between the flashing and roof and prevent water from backing up over the edge of the flashing.

If the flashing in a valley is too narrow or if it is corroded or broken, it will probably be necessary to replace it with new pieces of metal. This is not difficult in an open valley but is rather troublesome in a closed one.

In a closed valley covered with shingles, it is quite difficult to repair leaks in the flashing unless the metal pushed under the shingles to cover the leaky spots is folded into a wedge-shaped point. Folding makes it easier to push the sheets past obstacles such as nails. If nails interfere too much, they can be cut off under the shingle or pulled with a sharp cold chisel or nail ripper and later replaced with new nails. The size of the sheets to be used for flashing depends upon the pitch of the roof and the exposure of the shingles to the weather.

Insert a piece of flashing under top layer of first course of shingles at the eaves and over the top of the old flashing and slide it up until the upper point of the sheet is at least 2″ above the butts of the second course of shingles. Then insert another sheet under the second course of shingles, pushing it up on top of the old flashing. The lower point of this piece will show below the butts of the second course of shingles. Continue this process until the top of the valley has been reached or until all broken flashings have been

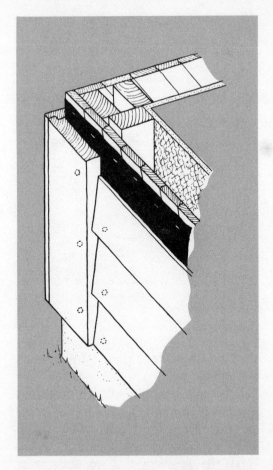

covered. If good material is used, this method makes a permanent repair and covers the cracks or holes that have rusted out in the angle of the original flashing.

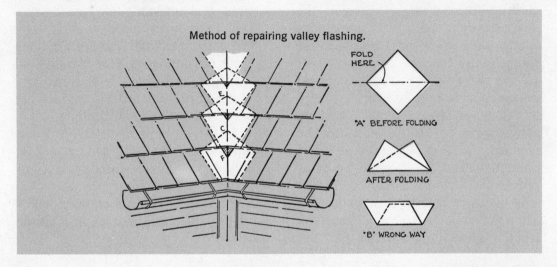

Method of repairing valley flashing.

FOLD HERE

"A" BEFORE FOLDING

AFTER FOLDING

"B" WRONG WAY

Make Walls Watertight

The wall joints most vulnerable to the entrance of water and moisture are those around windows and doors. Here, rain can be blown against the joints and forced into the house almost as though it were under pressure. Likewise, rain and melted snow run down the walls and can find their way through imperfectly sealed joints.

Without lasting protection, rain, melted snow, moisture, even wind, can enter your house, can destroy plaster, insulation, paint and wallpaper, can rot and weaken wooden framework, can cost you many times over the small sum you pay for the lasting protection of durable flashing.

Window Head Flashing

Steps 1 to 5 illustrate a proper and simple method of forming window head flashings.

In brick or stone veneer construction the flashing should be carried the full length of the lintel and at the ends it should turn up ½".

Where windows are wider than 44", use two sheets, lapping the ends a minimum of 3".

1. Cut a section of flashing 4" longer than the width of the window casing.
2. Flashing will extend horizontally out over window casing. When clapboard siding is used, flashing will extend vertically on wall a minimum of 4". When shingles are used, flashing will extend vertically on the wall 2" above the butt line of the succeeding course. Bend flashing lengthwise to form necessary vertical leg.

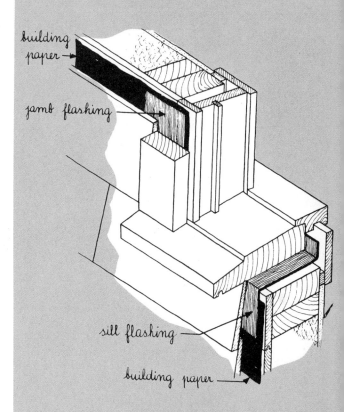

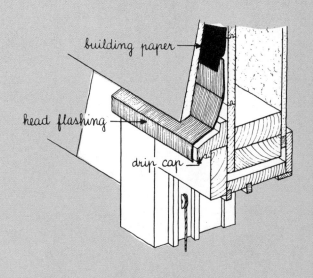

3. The flashing is held in place by nails along its upper edge. The outer edge of the horizontal leg is bent down over front of casing.

4. At side edges of casing, the metal should be slit to form tabs which are bent over the ends of the casing. First fold back the lower tabs, then fold down the upper tabs to cover them.

5. This procedure insures weathertight flashing, which is applicable to door heads as well as windows. For the sake of appearance, it is important to paint the exposed parts of such flashing.

Protect the Joints

1. Mark a full size sheet of flashing lengthwise down the middle. Then mark it crosswise into sections 9" long.

2. Cut along these lines to obtain pieces each 9" square.

3. Bend each piece lengthwise into a right angle along a line 4" from one edge (5" from the opposite edge).

4. The 5" legs will be placed on the roof, and the 4" legs will lie against the vertical wall.

5. Cut-away section—In laying the flashing, start at the eave line and work up. The separate pieces of flashing are set in between each course of shingles. Secure each piece to the roof boarding with a nail.

Flathead

This term, or flush head, is used to designate the head of a screw or bolt which can be set into a countersunk hole so that the top of the head rests level with the surface into which it was sunk.

Frequently, flathead screws are set so that the head is slightly below the surface. In this way, the cavity can be filled with wood filler or wood putty, which is sanded flush when dry. The final effect is the almost complete concealment of the screw head.

While it is possible to drive a flathead screw in soft wood so that its head is flush with the surface by using only a screwdriver, it is better to countersink the hole. In this way, there is less danger of cracking the head of the screw or splintering the wood.

Also see COUNTERSINK, BOLTS and SCREWS.

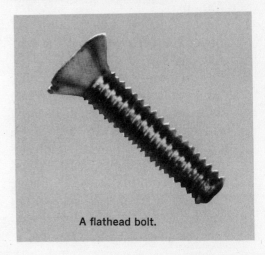

A flathead bolt.

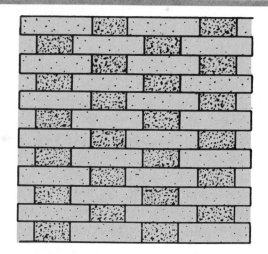

Flemish Bond

This is a form of bricklaying and consists of alternate headers and stretchers in every course. Each header is centered on the stretchers in the courses above and below.

Also see *BRICK*.

Float

A flat board or sheet of metal with a handle attached, used for concrete or plaster work. It is used to spread the concrete or plaster and to smooth the surface.

Also see *CONCRETE*.

Wood and steel floats are used for finishing concrete. The steel float produces a fine, smooth surface while the wood float produces a somewhat rougher texture.

Float Valve

Sometimes called a float, this is generally a hollow ball inside a toilet tank which controls the flow of water into the tank. The hollow ball floats on top of the water and, as the water rises, the ball connected to a control arm shuts the valve through which the water flows to fill the tank.

In recent years, the copper float has been displaced in some homes by floats made of polystyrene. In addition, inflated polystyrene in the shape of a block has been used as a float-valve.

Also see *DRAINAGE SYSTEMS* and *TOILET TANK REPAIRS*.

Float valve is part of the toilet tank water system controlling the inflow of water.

Floor Coverings, Maintenance

Both wood and concrete floors may be covered with linoleum, asphalt tile, and similar materials. Such coverings should be installed and maintained in accordance with the manufacturer's instructions, which usually include thorough cleaning and the application of protective wax coatings. Available in an almost limitless range of colors, these floor coverings will serve as a starting point for remodeling or changing the color scheme of a room.

Linoleum

Linoleum, whether for floor coverings, kitchen counter tops, walls, or other inside surfaces, will stay attractive longer and wear better if waxed and polished. A few simple rules for its care will be found useful: (1) dust daily; (2) use water sparingly; (3) clean with special linoleum cleaner, mild soapsuds, or mild detergent solution; (4) apply wax in a thin, even film; (5) rewax only as needed, usually not oftener than once a month; and (6) never use harsh abrasives other than fine steel wool to take off spots that are hard to remove.

No matter what type of wax is used, always start with a clean surface before waxing. There are some excellent linoleum cleaners which may be diluted with water in accordance with the manufacturer's directions. In using them, clean only a few square feet at a time, going over that area with a fresh cloth wrung out with clear, lukewarm water, and permit the surface to dry thoroughly and the wax to spread evenly.

Waxes that protect linoleum are essentially of two types: paste and liquid waxes with a volatile-solvent base, and self-polishing waxes with a water-emulsion base. They should be applied in very thin coats to avoid making the floor slippery.

Volatile-solvent waxes may be obtained in either paste or liquid form. The liquid is somewhat easier to apply than the paste because of the large proportion of solvent. Both paste and liquid are suitable for linoleum as well as for wood or concrete floors.

Paste wax should be applied with a slightly dampened soft cloth or with a wax applicator and allowed to dry, after which it should be polished to a lustrous finish. Liquid wax should be spread evenly over the cleaned surface with a lamb's-wool applicator in straight, parallel strokes. After drying for 30 minutes, it should be polished to a lustrous finish. Waxes of the organic-solvent type must not be used on asphalt tile because they soften and mar the surface of the tile.

Self-polishing or water-emulsion base waxes will give a protective coating if used on linoleum, rubber tile, cork, asphalt tile, mastic, and other flooring. The wax should be spread as thinly and evenly as possible with a lamb's-wool applicator or soft cloth mop in straight, parallel strokes. If properly applied it should dry to a hard, lustrous film in less

Photograph courtesy of Red Devil Tools.

than 30 minutes. Although not required, the gloss may be increased by a slight buffing after the wax becomes thoroughly dry.

A weighted floor brush or electric polishing machine does an excellent job with little effort. If a polisher is not part of the household equipment, it may be rented in many communities at nominal cost by the hour or the day. For a very hard surface, the linoleum should be given two or three coats of wax, making sure to let each coat dry for at least 30 minutes before polishing.

Care should be taken not to flood linoleum surfaces with water, since any water that seeps through the edges of seams may affect the cementing material and cause the backing to mildew or rot and edges of the linoleum to become loose and curled. Wiping up water as soon as it is spilled on waxed linoleum will keep light spots from appearing. Grease and other spots should be cleaned as quickly as possible, with a soft cloth or sponge wrung out of mild lukewarm soapsuds or mild detergent solution. Rinse by using a clean cloth wrung out of clear, lukewarm water. Floor oils and sweeping compound containing oil should not be used on linoleum, because these materials may leave a film of oil on the surface to collect dust and dirt.

Asphalt Tile

Asphalt tile may be used to cover both new and old concrete or wood floors and may be obtained in colors suitable for any room in the house. Impervious to water, the tiles are especially suitable for floors on which water is likely to be spilled, such as kitchens, laundries, and bathrooms; they also prove attractive and satisfactory for basement recreation rooms and enclosed porches.

When installing this type of flooring, always obtain a few extra tiles for replacement or testing, because it may be difficult to match them exactly later on. Missing tiles or those that have become broken or marred should be replaced by cementing new ones into place.

Mastic floor covering of the asphalt type has asphalt, bitumen, or resin as the base and will give excellent service if given proper care. There are some "do's" and "don'ts" which are very important. Cleaners and polishes containing abrasives, oils, or organic solvents, such as gasoline, turpentine, or carbon tetrachloride, should not be used to clean asphalt-base coverings. Never use unknown cleaning preparations on asphalt tile without testing them first, unless they are recommended by the manufacturer of the flooring.

To test a cleaning or polishing preparation for use on asphalt tile, moisten a white cloth with the preparation and rub over the surface of a spare tile. If the color of the tile shows on the cloth, the preparation has acted as a solvent, dissolving the surface of the tile, and is not safe to use.

Asphalt tile floors may be washed with neutral soap and lukewarm water in much the same manner as linoleum, except that water will not harm the tile unless permitted to stand and seep under edges enough to loosen them from the floor. After cleaning and drying, the care of asphalt tile floors is similar to that recommended for linoleum with one very important exception: Never use paste wax or liquid wax that has a solvent base on asphalt tile—these waxes will soften the tile and mar the surface.

Water-emulsion or self-polishing waxes that are free from oils are suitable and safe for asphalt tile. They should be spread as thinly as possible on the surface of the floor with lamb's-wool applicator. Use straight, parallel strokes in one direction only. In a short time, approximately 30 minutes, the wax should dry to a hard, lustrous finish. While these waxes are self-polishing to a degree, the appearance of the floor will be improved by a light buffing. Before polishing, however, the wax should be completely dry.

Wax should be renewed at intervals, depending upon the severity of wear, but it is not necessary to re-wax as long as the floor responds to polishing. Daily dusting and occasional machine polishing will eliminate the need of mopping and extend the life of the wax coating.

Photograph courtesy of Red Devil Tools.

Floors

Photo courtesy of Flintkote Flooring and Spring Mills

Floors, like walls, are extensive and not easy to change. When finishing a new addition to your home— extra bedrooms in the attic, a family recreation center in the basement or a garage converted into a den—you should choose your floor material carefully and wisely. Floors are meant to be walked on, less often to be run, jumped or danced on. They must also support the weight of furniture as well as provide comfort.

What are the attributes of a 'good' floor?

1. It should be durable, able to take the daily punishment without cracking, disintegrating or wearing noticeably.

2. It should be easy to maintain. It should not be necessary to refinish frequently because of scratch marks, or to scour daily to remove shoe prints.

3. It should be resilient; in other words, have a bounce when you walk on it. A 'stiff' floor without some spring is very tiring if you stand on your feet on it for any prolonged period or do considerable walking to and fro as the homemaker must in her kitchen.

4. It should be sound-absorbing in that it should deaden noise; although walls and ceilings offer better possibilities for absorbing noise, the floor should help and not hinder.

This section is confined to hard-surface flooring as opposed to soft floor coverings (carpets and rugs). Here are some of the hard-surface

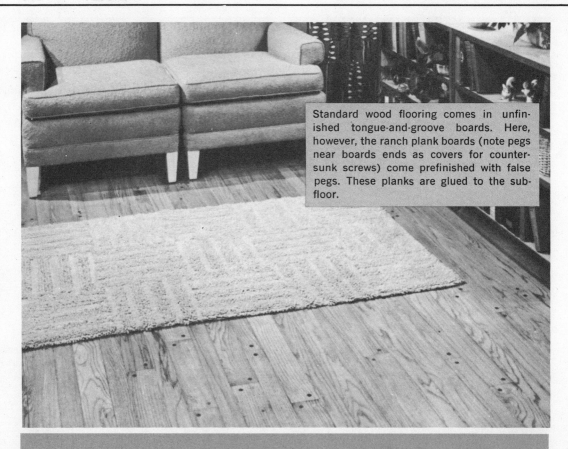

Standard wood flooring comes in unfinished tongue-and-groove boards. Here, however, the ranch plank boards (note pegs near boards ends as covers for countersunk screws) come prefinished with false pegs. These planks are glued to the subfloor.

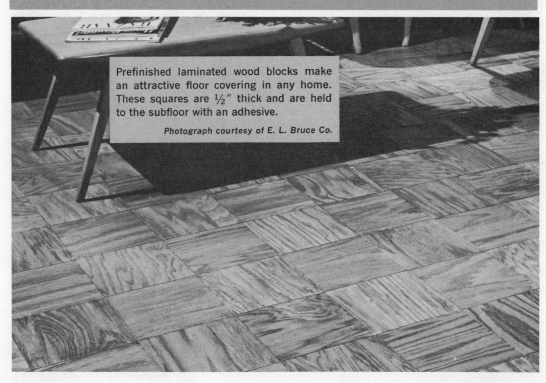

Prefinished laminated wood blocks make an attractive floor covering in any home. These squares are ½" thick and are held to the subfloor with an adhesive.

Photograph courtesy of E. L. Bruce Co.

Vinyl-asbestos tiles in spatter pattern can be installed below grade as well as on ground level and suspended floors. These are rugged blocks able to withstand the use and abuse in a child's room.

Photograph courtesy of Armstrong Cork Co.

Old fashioned linoleum is given a new look with the addition of bright metallic chips. Large cocoa and black squares combine to make a high style room.

Photograph courtesy of Mastic Tile Corp.

flooring materials for use in the home.

ASPHALT TILE—It can be used directly over concrete or wood floors and generally comes in 9″x9″ squares although other sizes and shapes are available. These tiles are easy to maintain but too often are noisy. Furthermore, they become brittle in cold weather and soft with heat. They cannot be used where they come into direct contact with the elements.

CONCRETE—This is the least expensive of all flooring materials but is not too attractive. It is generally covered with another surface: wood, asphalt tiles or carpets and rugs. It is exceedingly durable but cold unless radiant-heated. It has no resiliency.

LINOLEUM—Available in rolls and in squares, this floor covering material is moderately easy to main-

Another unusual treatment given ordinary asphalt tiles. A parquet effect is obtained by the scored lines in each block and with the blocks set at right angles to one another.

Photograph courtesy of Mastic Tile Corp.

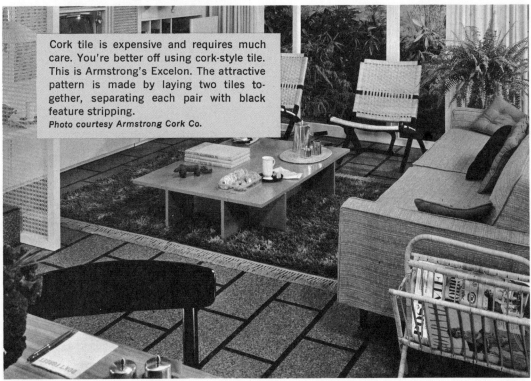

Cork tile is expensive and requires much care. You're better off using cork-style tile. This is Armstrong's Excelon. The attractive pattern is made by laying two tiles together, separating each pair with black feature stripping.

Photo courtesy Armstrong Cork Co.

tain. To increase the wear life and maintain the appearance of linoleum, it is necessary to wax fairly frequently.

RUBBER—This highly durable flooring material is very resilient and easy to maintain. It comes in a wide range of colors and is greaseproof. Generally, the handyman uses rubber in tile form although roll goods are available.

VINYL-ASBESTOS—This composition tile can be used anywhere asphalt tile is used in the home. It is highly durable and easy to maintain. It has more resilience than asphalt and is not as easily affected by cold and heat.

VINYL—This floor covering usually comes in tile form and can be purchased in many different colors and textures. It is very easy to maintain and particularly practical in kitchens and bathrooms.

WOOD—The standard floor covering found in practically every home is available as individual, unfinished tongue-and-groove boards or in prefinished blocks or boards In some instances, it is possible to use plywood or hardboard as flooring material. Wood is resilient and warm.

FLAGSTONE—Used in the proper setting, flagstones make attractive and durable entrance halls

Using different colored tiles to form unusual patterns adds to the decorative effect of a tile floor.

Photograph courtesy of Rubber Manufacturers Association.

Dramatic floor treatment is all that it takes to make even an entry way of postage-stamp proportions say a big welcome to your home.

Large tiles, 12"x12", make a striking pattern in a room. Here confetti pattern tile is used in two contrasting colors.
Photograph courtesy of Mastic Tile Corp.

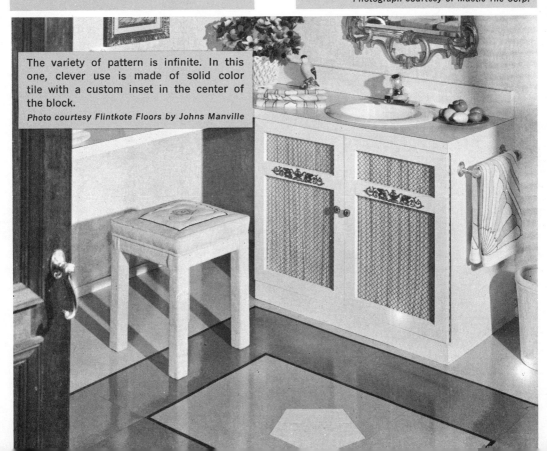

The variety of pattern is infinite. In this one, clever use is made of solid color tile with a custom inset in the center of the block.
Photo courtesy Flintkote Floors by Johns Manville

Floors—Tiles

Floor tiles are easy for the handyman to install. Today, there are tiles made of many different materials which can be used in every room of the house. These are, however, limitations on certain types of tiles which cannot be laid below ground (that is, below ground level) while others are not recommended for areas where the tiles are likely to be stained (for example, in the kitchen).

Asphalt tiles, rubber tiles, cork tiles, vinyl tiles, and vinyl-asbestos tiles can be used for any do-it-yourself project. There are many different colors, patterns and sizes available.

Before you lay any tiles, it is necessary to prepare the floor surface. Tiles set over uneven floors may crack or show ridges where the floor is uneven. Therefore, follow preparation steps carefully so that your job, when completed, is worth the effort.

Among the tools you will need are: a serrated paste spreader, a sharp flooring knife, chalk and chalk-line, ruler or yardstick, a steel straight edge to guide the cutting knife, dividers, trowel for spreading the adhesive and a carpenter's square. You will also need a hammer and a nail set if a felt lining is needed under the tiles you are laying.

Among the materials you will need are tile adhesive and tiles. In some instances, you will also need

How To Install Floor Tiles

1. It is best to center the floor tiles by starting in the middle of the room. Mark center line down the length of the room and another at right angles to it across the room. When you start the tiles afterwards, lay the tiles at the intersection of the two center lines.

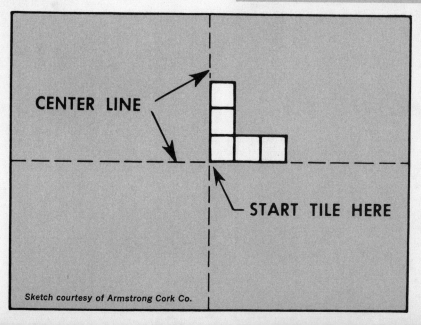

CENTER LINE

START TILE HERE

Sketch courtesy of Armstrong Cork Co.

felt lining and linoleum paste to adhere this lining to the original floor.

No matter what type of floor tile you plan to use, the technique for laying the tiles is practically the same. Certain tiles require special adhesives and it is, therefore, best to follow manufacturers' instructions, using the following as a guide.

If tiles are to be placed on concrete, it is necessary to have a perfectly smooth surface. There are special mastics which are spread over the floor and evened-off so that all indentations are filled. The tiles can be laid directly over the concrete.

On wooden floors, however, it is usually necessary to lay a felt lining over the boards to prevent the board edges from eventually showing through the tiles. Unless the wooden floor is perfectly smooth and all the joints between the boards properly filled, a felt lining is recommended for under the tiles. Certain tiles require this lining no matter how smooth the floor. Therefore, check the manufacturers' literature before starting your floor project.

Furthermore, when laying tiles in a room with a baseboard, it is best to remove the shoe mold (See *BASE-BOARD*) by prying it off with a floor or glazier's chisel so that the edges of the tile can be concealed afterwards when the molding is replaced.

2. The center lines are best made with a chalk line. If you don't have a chalk line (a useful, inexpensive accessory available in any store selling floor tiles or hardware), you can use string with marking chalk. Tack the two ends in place and snap the cord; this will leave a chalk line where you want it.

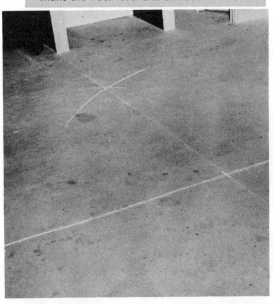

3. Here is a chalk line across the room and down the length of the room on a concrete floor in the basement. This smooth concrete requires no further preparation; the tiles can be laid directly over it. If it were uneven, however, it would be necessary to use a special mastic filler to make the floor level and smooth.

4. When working on a wooden floor, a felt lining is frequently necessary. Linoleum adhesive is spread over the floor with a notched trowel and the cut sheets of felt are laid over the adhesive.

5. After the center lines have been marked, start in one segment of the room and apply the tile adhesive over the floor. Spread the adhesive evenly so that there are no bare spots or lumps anywhere in the work area.

6. The tiles are then set over the adhesive starting with the first tile aligned with the two center lines. Continue laying the tiles so that the edges abutt the center line, which is used as a guide.

Photograph courtesy of Armstrong Cork Co.

7. Always work from the uncovered portion of the floor. Place each tile in position; don't slide them. This will prevent the adhesive from oozing up between the tiles joints. If, however, any adhesive does ooze up, wipe it off immediately with a clean, damp cloth.

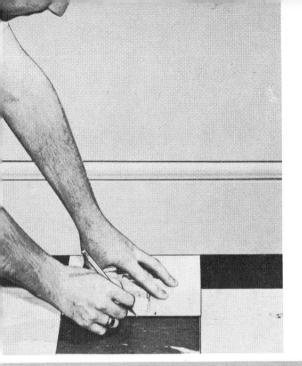

8. After laying all the tiles in one section of the floor, you can lay those in the other sections, leaving the incompleted portions until the end. To fill in the space between the last complete tile and the wall, set a tile over the one already in place. Then place another tile over it and against the wall. With a pencil or a scribing tool, mark the lower tile to size and cut it.

9. Cut the tile to size with a flooring knife and a steel straight edge. Set the tile on a piece of wood for cutting so that you don't mar the floor. If you have an assistant, you can cut the tiles to size while your assistant marks them.

10. Around door frames and other projections in the room, you might find a pair of dividers exceedingly helpful in determining the exact size and shape to cut the tiles. Mark the location of the last full tile on the floor and then measure the amount needed for the filler tile. Transfer measurements from floor with dividers to the tile and then cut to shape.

Photograph courtesy of Armstrong Cork Co.

11. Asphalt tile is easier to cut if heated slightly. You can use a sun lamp or heat lamp to warm the tiles.

12. A blowtorch, used carefully, is another way to heat the asphalt tiles before you cut them to shape and size.

13. Special cutting is often necessary to fit a tile around a pipe or other object protruding from the floor, such as a sink leg which cannot be removed. It is best to make a paper pattern and then trace this onto a tile. Then tiles can be cut with scissors.

Photograph courtesy of Armstrong Cork Co.

14. It is sometimes best to heat the tile after it has been cut so that it will be easier to bend around an immovable object. Heating the tile for a few seconds over the kitchen range makes the tile pliable and easier to bend.

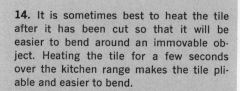

15. Twist the heated tile and slide it around the object so that the straight-cut side is nearest the wall where it won't be easily seen. Replace the shoe mold (see **Baseboard**) after the tiles have been set in place.

Luxurious vinyl tile lets you dwell in marble halls, 70's style. With imagination, tile can provide all kinds of decorative ideas. Here, the statuary appears to be in its own niche, in reality a tiled area on the wall. Tile accents have also been added in this beautiful room by using it for some wall areas and on the serving shelf at left.

Photo courtesy Flintkote Vintal Tile

Easy do-it-yourself project is this floor of nine-inch Peel & Stick tiles with self-adhesive backs. You do just what the name tells you—peel protective paper backing, exposing ready-to-use adhesive, and stick it to the floor. No special preparation is required. Just make sure the floor is level, clean and dry. Pattern seen here is Flintkote's Colonial Stone.

Photo courtesy The Flintkote Company

Laying Self-Adhesive Tiles

To make life simpler for the handyman or the handywoman, there are floor tiles available which come already prepared with adhesive. This speeds the floor tile laying job and, when a felt lining is not needed, eliminates part of the mess sometimes encountered.

1. To lay Peel & Stick tile, start working from the center of the room. Snap chalk lines to provide starting guides.

2. Without removing paper backing, lay a row of loose tile along the chalk line from the center point to one side wall and one end wall. If the distance to the wall is less than 3", snap a new chalk line to allow more room.

3. Remove the paper backing only when actually ready to apply the tile. Start placing squares at center point, following chalk lines. Don't slide tile on floor. Set in place with one edge, then press down firmly.

4. Butt each tile squarely to the previous one. Corners should meet exactly. Don't apply pressure until you're sure the tile is correctly placed, because once applied, the adhesive makes the tile difficult to move.

5. To fit around obstacles or at edges, cut tile with shears or sharp linoleum knife and straightedge. Cut on paper side of tile. Around obstructions like this, it's smart to use a paper pattern.

Floors—Wood

Photograph courtesy of E. L. Bruce Co.

Wood floors can be secured directly over the joists in a house or even over concrete. A subfloor, however, is used for added strength.

Today, most subfloors are made of plywood which is nailed across the joists. The finished flooring is attached over the subfloor. Normally, tongue-and-groove boards are nailed to the subfloor. It is necessary to press the boards close together so that gaps between boards are at a minimum. Flooring nails, driven at a diagonal through the tongue, are concealed when the next board is set into place.

These tongue-and-groove boards come prefinished as well as unfinished. If you have a perfectly smooth subfloor, you should en-counter no difficulty in laying a wood floor. However, covering of uneven subfloors should be left to the professional.

Although moderately expensive, prefinished wood squares can be used as the finished flooring. These blocks are held in place by an adhesive. Note instructions later in this section.

Tongue-and-groove boards are secured by blind nailing. A flooring nail is driven diagonally through the tongue of the board into the subfloor. When the next piece is added, the groove conceals the nail head.

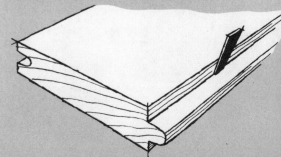

To keep the boards together tightly when nailing, it is best to use a pinch bar and a wedge (piece of flooring with one edge square).

Another method to keep the boards together when nailing is to fasten a block to the subfloor and use a wooden wedge to press against the flooring boards.

After the floor boards are nailed in place, the joint between the floor and wall are covered with a molding, a baseboard. See **Baseboard.**

Nailing prefinished ranch type flooring in place. Note that a waterproof paper has been laid over the subfloor.

Photograph courtesy of E. L. Bruce Co.

How To Install Laminated Oak Blocks

TOOLS NEEDED
Tape measure or rule
Chalk line and chalk
Carpenter's hammer
Broom
Hand saw and coping or
    band saw
Priming brush or squeegee
    (for applying primer)
Coke or charcoal burner (for
    heating mastic)
Notched trowel with 1/4"
    teeth on 3/8" centers, for
    spreading mastic)

SUBFLOORS

Laminated blocks can be installed over subfloors of concrete, dressed and matched wood, or plywood. Under certain conditions, old surface floors of wood or asphalt tile are equally suitable. Depending on type, subfloors should answer the following specifications:

Concrete—Subfloors should be sound, level, dry, smooth, and clean. Remove grease or oil stains with a

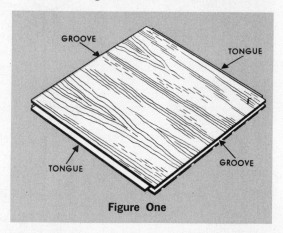

GROOVE

TONGUE

TONGUE

GROOVE

Figure One

Laying Prefinished Wood Squares

1. The wood block is set in place over the center line after the mastic is applied over the floor.

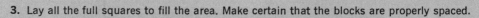

2. Additional blocks are set in place with tongues and grooves interlocking.

3. Lay all the full squares to fill the area. Make certain that the blocks are properly spaced.

4. Fill in the remaining areas by cutting blocks to the required size and setting them in place.

Photographs courtesy of E. L. Bruce Co.

solution of industrial lye, using about one pound of lye to each three gallons of water. Level high spots with a terrazzo grinder, Carborundum stone, or hammer and chisel. Fill low areas to general subfloor level with a good-quality concrete patching mix, according to directions on the container.

Wood or Plywood—Newly-constructed wood subfloors should be of dressed and matched boards not over 6″ wide. New plywood subfloors should be well-nailed at all edges and through the center. Rough edges should be sanded smooth. Either type subfloor must be sound, level, and well-nailed.

Renail old wood subfloors or old surface flooring where neces-

sary, and level any raised edges by rough-sanding. Roughsand old surface floors to remove varnish, paint, shellac, or wax.

Asphalt Tile—Laminated blocks may be laid directly over old asphalt tile if the tile is not crumbled, loose, or otherwise in poor condition. Make sure that tiles are firmly bonded; if not, remove all tile down to subfloor level, and sand or scrape the subfloor to remove all traces of old tile cement.

If tiles are well bonded, roughsand the surface to remove wax. This may also be done satisfactorily by cleaning with water and a good-quality household scouring powder. Allow ample drying time afterward.

Remove base shoe molding and

doorway thresholds before beginning installation of blocks over old surface of any type.

Dampproofing the Subfloor

Laminated blocks are unusually stable under adverse moisture conditions. They do not expand unduly except when subjected to "flooding" or actual immersion in water.

No dampproofing between subfloor and surface floor is necessary where blocks are to be laid over wood or plywood subfloors or over a concrete slab subfloor suspended above ground level. Do not use a paper underlayment of any kind over subfloors of these types.

However, a full two-ply, dampproofing membrane should be installed over concrete subfloors at ground level or in direct contact with the ground where capillary moisture (seepage of water upward through the concrete) is suspected. Check for capillary moisture as follows:

Put 5 to 6 tablespoonfuls of powdered calcium chloride on the concrete; build a "well" of putty about 1" high around the chemical, then cover with a piece of glass 8" or 10" square. Seal edges with putty to keep out air.

If, within 24 hours, water droplets appear on the glass or the chemical shows signs of caking, capillary moisture is present. A competent waterproofing contractor should then be employed to install a dampproofing membrane, as follows, before laying any floor:

(1) Sweep the surface and prime with asphalt primer.

(2) Coat the subfloor with hot asphalt or with Bruce Everbond "X".

(3) While asphalt or mastic is

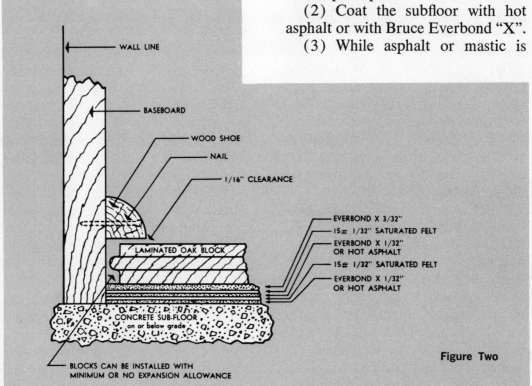

WALL LINE

BASEBOARD

WOOD SHOE

NAIL

1/16" CLEARANCE

EVERBOND X 3/32"
15# 1/32" SATURATED FELT
EVERBOND X 1/32"
OR HOT ASPHALT
15# 1/32" SATURATED FELT
EVERBOND X 1/32"
OR HOT ASPHALT

LAMINATED OAK BLOCK

CONCRETE SUB-FLOOR
on or below grade

BLOCKS CAN BE INSTALLED WITH
MINIMUM OR NO EXPANSION ALLOWANCE

Figure Two

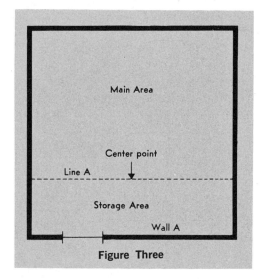

Main Area

Center point

Line A

Storage Area

Wall A

Figure Three

hot, embed a layer of 15-pound as-phalt-saturated felt, starting with a half-sheet at one wall and butting all seams. Mop firmly to press out wrinkles and blisters.

(4) Cover felt with another coating of hot asphalt or mastic and embed second layer of felt. Start with a full sheet instead of a half sheet so that seams of the first layer are covered.

Priming the Subfloor

Concrete subfloors that have not been waterproofed should be primed with asphalt primer before spreading mastic to settle dust and provide the best possible bonding surface.

Priming is unnecessary on sub-floors other than concrete. Do not, under any circumstances, prime as-phalt tile. Remove dust on asphalt tile by mopping with warm water, then allowing to dry completely. Remove dust on wood or plywood subfloors by thorough sweeping.

Laying Out Working Lines

The following instructions deal with the installation of blocks in a square pattern without regard to balanced borders at walls. Installation should begin nearest the wall containing the main entranceway.

1. (Figure 3): From Wall A, measure off at two points an equal distance sufficient to provide a convenient initial working space and storage area for materials. This measurement should be carefully calculated to allow a full or nearly full block in the doorway. After de-termining the distance desired, check by laying a row of blocks loosely on the subfloor from the point estab-lished through the doorway; the final block should reach past the center of the door jamb.

2. Snap a chalk line, Line A in Figure 3, from wall to wall across these two points. This line should be parallel to Wall A.

Applying the Mastic

Everbond "X" Mastic requires heating, and is applied to the sub-floor while hot. Note: Do not at-tempt to lay blocks in mastic when room temperature is less than 45°F. A temperature of about 70° is pre-ferable.

1. Heat Everbond "X" to a liquid consistency over a coke or charcoal burner or over an outside fire, first removing the cover. Stir while heating. Do not allow mastic to boil, and guard against accidental contact with water to avoid uncon-trollable frothing. If using pails of mastic, keep one pail over heat while a second is in use; if using drums, dip hot mastic from drum to pail for ease in handling.

2. Begin applying mastic to sub-

Figure Four

floor at the wall opposite the entranceway. Pour from pail and spread evenly with a notched trowel with ¼″ teeth on ⅜″ centers to gain the desired depth of ³⁄₃₂″. Hold trowel in a nearly vertical position while in use, (Figure 4).

3. Let mastic dry and "set" until a glaze appears on the surface.

Laying the Blocks

After mastic has set, begin laying blocks as directed below. When laying blocks see that edges of blocks coincide with the line rather than tongues or grooves, to secure true alignment.

When placing blocks in position, insert groove over tongue or tongue into groove and drop block lightly into place. Tap on the exposed sides to complete positioning. Do not attempt to slide blocks into place; mastic will pile up on the leading edge, impeding the fit. Use mineral spirits to remove any mastic adhering to the surface of blocks by accident.

1. Locate the approximate center point of Line A.

2. (Figure 5): Lay Block No. 1 on Line A at this point. Place this initial block with a grooved side along the working line. This is the key block; make sure it is positioned correctly to make exact alignment of additional blocks easier.

3. (Figure 6): Next lay Blocks 2 and 3 on either side of Block 1, fitting tongues and grooves as required. Align these blocks carefully with Line A and with each other.

4. (Figure 6): Place Block 4 directly over Block 1, establishing a "pyramid" pattern extending from Line A into the main area of the room.

5. (Figure 7): Lay Blocks 5, 6, 7, 8, and 9 around the pyramid pattern established in Step 4. Make sure that Blocks 5 and 9 are positioned exactly on Line A, and that Block 7 is perfectly aligned with Block 4.

6. (Figure 7): Continue laying

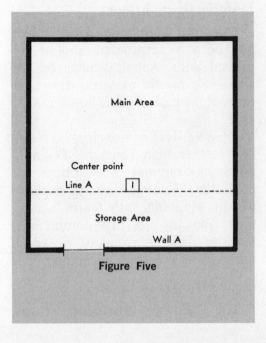

Figure Five

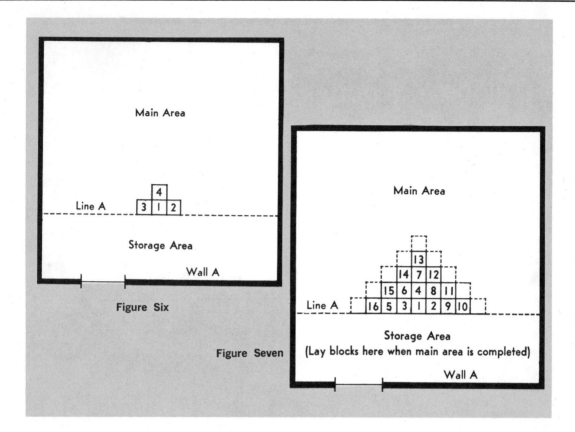

Figure Six

Figure Seven

Blocks 10 through 16 around the pyramid in the manner described in step 5. Follow with additional blocks in this fashion until walls are reached. Trim part blocks to fit at wall lines, around pipes and other projections, and around jambs at doorways. Let border blocks extend as far as possible into door openings.

No expansion allowance is necessary at walls or around projecting obstacles since the laminated blocks are relatively stable even under poor moisture conditions; lay blocks as snugly as possible against all vertical surfaces.

7. When the main area has been partly laid, move all materials onto the completed portion of the floor and spread mastic over storage area between Line A and Wall A (Figure 7). Then continue filling in main area as instructed in step 6. When main area is completed and freshly-spread mastic has "set," lay blocks along Line A until storage area is covered. Follow the same procedure as before. Cut part blocks, if necessary, to fit along Wall A.

8. When floor is completed, install new factory-finished base shoe mold of proper size, or re-install old molding.

If there is any appreciable difference in elevation between the new floor of laminated blocks and old floors in adjoining rooms, overcome by using a special 7/16"x1½" factory finished oak nosing strip obtainable through any lumber dealer.

Floors—Wood: How To Finish

When wood floors show signs of extreme wear or become spotty, it is necessary to remove the old finish and apply a new one. This job can be done by the handyman with tools rented from the local hardware store.

The job can be broken down into three phases: first, removal of the old finish; second, the cleaning up or the removal of dirt; and third, the application of the finish.

Several types of floor finishes can be used. There is the traditional shellac or varnish plus other materials, such as penetrating oil stains with wax or hard surface finishes, such as Fabulon, which require no waxing.

Here, in this section, are the details for refinishing old floors, how to finish new floors and information about floor finishes.

How To Refinish Old Floors

PREPARING THE SURFACE —The primary requisite for a good job is the proper preparation of the wood surface. Regardless of the finishing material used, a smooth, clean wood surface before the finish is applied is essential if Grade A results are to be obtained. After all, it must be remembered that the finish itself simply covers and protects the wood and cannot be expected to correct unlevel areas or rough spots.

"Gloss" or that "brilliant gleam"

A most important step in preparing old floors for refinishing is to make certain no nail heads protrude. They'll rip up the sandpaper if they do, to say nothing of looking ugly. Counterset each nail below the surface and fill the hole with wood putty.

Another important step in floor refinishing is the removal of old baseboard corner moldings, to allow the sanding machine to get right up to the wall. Old moldings may break unless removed carefully. Save yourself work later on and remove them slowly—in one piece.

Photos courtesy Pierce & Stevens

is created by the reflection of light rays. The smoother the surface, the greater the reflection; the greater the reflection, the greater the gloss. Furthermore, smooth floors are far easier to clean and to keep clean.

To prepare old wood floors for correct finishing, all previous finishes must be completely removed, and the surface must be bare, clean, smooth, dust-free and dry. Power sanding is by far the most widely used method of removing old finishes and is generally considered the most practical and effective, although paint and varnish removers are sometimes used.

PROPER SANDING A "MUST"

—When using the sanding method, don't try to save time by sanding too fast or by ignoring any steps which might seem unnecessary. Try to remember that success or failure of the final job depends on how well you accomplish the sanding operation, and that 5 or 10 minutes apparently saved by skipping just one step might completely nullify all of the time, effort and money invested in the job.

USE OF LIQUID REMOVERS

—When considering the use of paint and varnish remover for removing old floor finishes, remember there are two basic types of removers . . .

Use the disc edge sander along baseboards, on stair treads, and in other areas inaccessible to the drum sander. Use closed coat sandpaper only.

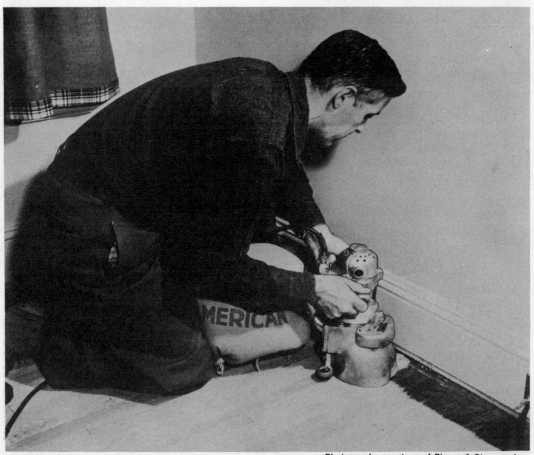

Photographs courtesy of Pierce & Stevens, Inc.

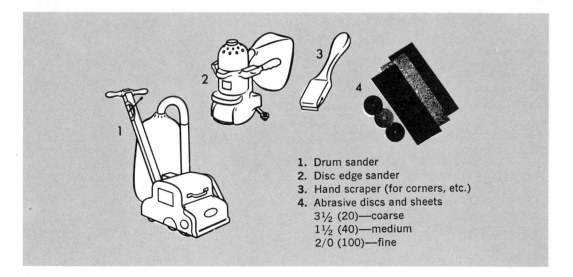

1. Drum sander
2. Disc edge sander
3. Hand scraper (for corners, etc.)
4. Abrasive discs and sheets
   3½ (20)—coarse
   1½ (40)—medium
   2/0 (100)—fine

viscous and non-viscous. The principal difference between the two occurs in the viscous type, which contains a retardant bodying agent such as wax, paraffin or oil. This ingredient retards the evaporation of the solvents and allows more time to soften the old finish. This is an advantage where vertical or irregular surfaces are involved. These viscous-type removers, however, require a neutralizing after-rinse to remove all traces of the bodying agent which may, if not thoroughly removed, retard the drying or otherwise adversely affect the new finish after it is applied.

Non-viscous removers contain no such retarding agents and require no after-rinse. Though non-viscous removers have a faster rate of evaporation, they are usually preferred for removing old finishes from horizontal surfaces such as floors. Because the surface is flat, there is sufficient time for the remover to soften the finish, and the elimination of the after-rinse saves considerable time and effort. It is advisable, however, first to remove

any wax or grease with a water-soluble wax-removing powder (such as *Wax-Off* or equivalent) before attempting to remove the old finish with a non-viscous remover.

SANDING—Before the floors are sanded, the following steps should be observed:

1. Wear clean, soft-soled shoes.
2. Remove all furniture, pictures, shades, etc., from the room.
3. Fasten loose boards, replace broken or badly split boards, and counter-sink all protruding nail heads.
4. Remove base shoe moldings (optional). This facilitates sanding close to the wall, but requires careful handling to prevent breaking of the molding.
5. Open all windows, and close doors of adjoining rooms.

Next, follow the three basic sanding steps:

First sanding: The purpose of this initial sanding operation is to remove the old finish down to the bare wood. Using 3½ (20 grit—open-coat) sandpaper in the machine, pass

Chart of Sanding Operations—Old Floors

FLOOR	OPERATION	TYPE OF PAPER	
Covered with Varnish, Shellac, Paint, etc.	First cut	Coarse	3½ (20)
	Second Cut	Medium	1½ (40)
	Finish Sanding	Fine	2/0 (100)

straight to the opposite wall. Then pass the sander back along the same path. This return pass enables the machine to pick up the dust created by the first pass. Be sure to follow this procedure throughout the entire sanding schedule.

Each complete pass (from wall to wall and return) should overlap previous pass by 2″ to 3″.

Although some refinishers prefer diagonal sanding on the first cut, remember that any criss-cross or cross-grain sanding must be followed by lengthwise sanding with the same grit paper.

Second sanding: The purpose of this sanding operation is to remove

the drum sander slowly over the floor lengthwise with the floor boards, starting at one wall and moving

Never stop the forward motion of the sanding machine while the sanding drum is in contact with the floor. This is particularly important when sanding soft woods such as pine with coarse open-coat paper in the sanding machine. If the machine is allowed to rest heavily in one spot, deep cuts, scratches or gouges in the wood will result. If severe, such indentations are impossible to level with the remaining floor area in the subsequent sanding operations.

the roughness caused by the coarse sandpaper used in the initial sanding operation. Use 1½ (40) paper in the machine, moving at a slow to medium rate of walking speed, pass drum sander over the floor length-wise with the floor boards. Each complete pass should overlap previous pass from 2″ to 3″.

Final sanding: The purpose of this sanding operation is to obtain a perfectly smooth surface, the primary requisite for a Grade A finished job, regardless of the finishing material used. Although the floor may appear smooth after the second sanding, the final sanding is most essential to insure proper surface preparation.

Always use 2/0 (100 grit) paper for this operation. Pass the drum sander over the floor length-wise with the floor boards. The rate of walking speed may be increased considerably during this operation. Each complete pass should overlap previous pass from 2″ to 3″.

Equip the disc edge sander with the same grit paper as the drum sander, and in the same sequence . . . that is, after using 3½ paper in the drum sander, also use 3½ paper for the disc edge sanding, before the second cut with the drum sander is made.

DUSTING — Remove all dust from the floor with a vacuum cleaner, dry cloth, brush or dry mop; include also window ledges, baseboards and any other surfaces where dust appears.

APPLYING THE FINISH — After the sanding and dusting operations are completed, the floors, old or new, are ready for the application of the finish. This operation should follow as soon as possible, since moisture from the air may enter the open pores of bare wood. If freshly-sanded floors remain exposed for any considerable length of time, the wood pores may absorb an excessive amount of moisture. Later, this moisture may work its way upwards through the pores and attack the finish from beneath, resulting in objectionable "white spots," chipping, peeling, grain-raising, etc.

How To Finish New Floors

Principally because of its attractive grain patterns and its durability, oak is the most widely-used hardwood for new floors. Other hardwoods

Remove all dust from the floor with a vacuum cleaner.
Photographs courtesy of Pierce & Stevens, Inc.

such as beech, birch and maple are also used, and in some areas softwood flooring such as pine and fir is popular.

PREPARING THE SURFACE —Regardless of kind, wood flooring when received from the lumber yard is milled but not sanded. Thus new flooring must be sanded after installation to prepare the surface for correct finishing. As in the case of refinishing old floors, proper sanding in finishing new floors is of paramount importance.

SANDING—*First cut:* The purpose of this sanding operation is to obtain a level, even surface. If the sub-floor was in good condition, and the new top-flooring properly installed, No. 1 (50 grit) paper may be used for the first sanding operation. A coarser grade, No. 2 (36 grit) is recommended if the floor is noticeably uneven. NOTE: Open coat abrasive paper should never be used for sanding new floors.

Using the correct grade of sandpaper in the sanding machine (see chart), pass the drum sander slowly over the floor sanding lengthwise with the floor boards, starting at one wall and moving straight to the opposite wall. Then pass the sander back along the same pass. This return pass enables the machine to pick up the dust created by the first pass. (Be sure to follow this procedure throughout the entire sanding schedule).

Each complete pass (from wall to wall and return) should overlap previous pass by 2″ to 3″.

FINAL SANDING: Always use 2/0 (100 grit) paper for this operation. Pass the drum sander over the floor lengthwise with the floor boards. The rate of walking speed may be increased considerably during this operation. Each complete pass should overlap previous pass from 2″ to 3″.

Equip the disc edge sander with the same grit paper as the drum sander and in the same sequence . . . that is, after using No. 1 paper in the drum sander, also use No. 1 paper for the disc edge sanding, before the second cut with the drum

Chart of Sanding Operations—New Floors				
FLOOR	**OPERATION**		**GRADE OF SANDPAPER**	
Hardwood Oak, Maple, Beech, Birch	First Cut	Uneven Floor	Medium-Coarse	2 (36)
		Ordinary Floor	Fine	1 (50)
	Final Sanding		Extra Fine	2/0 (100)
Softwood Pine Fir	First Cut	Uneven Floor	Medium-Fine	1½ (40)
		Ordinary Floor	Fine	1 (50)
	Final Sanding		Extra Fine	2/0 (100)

sander is made.

Use the disc sander along baseboards, on stair treads, and in other areas inaccessible to the drum sander. Use the hand-scraper in areas inaccessible to the disc edge sander as behind radiator pipes.

DUSTING — Remove all dust from the floor with a vacuum cleaner, dry cloth, brush or dry mop; include also window ledges, baseboards, and any other surfaces where dust appears.

APPLYING THE FINISH—Follow same procedure as when refinishing old floors.

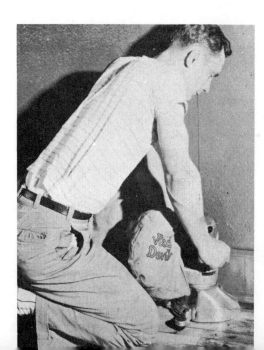

Floor Finishes

SHELLAC—Shellac is fast-drying and relatively easy to apply. It is packed in two principle types . . . white shellac and orange shellac. Upon application, white shellac darkens the wood less than orange shellac and is usually applied where it is desired to retain as much as possible of the natural tint of the wood. Shellac is usually packaged as a 4-pound or 5-pound cut (a mixture of 4 or 5 pounds of shellac gum dissolved in one gallon of denatured ethyl alcohol). A 2–2½ pound cut (approximately 1/3 reduction of a 4-pound cut) is usually recommended for floors.

Shellac should be fresh when purchased and carefully protected from exposure to sunlight and air to avoid the possibility of deterioration. Therefore, only quantities sufficient for present purposes should be purchased at any given time. To avoid contamination in direct contact with tin, shellac manufacturers usually package in specially-lined metal containers or glass bottles. Any unused portion should be returned to the original container and never left overnight in any other metal container.

Until recently, the use of wood filler on oak floors prior to the application of shellac was almost invariably recommended. However, after laboratory and field tests proved up to 50% longer life when applied to the bare wood (no filler) in thin coats, many shellac manufacturers now consider the use of wood filler optional. On the other hand, many professional finishers still use filler to obtain a satisfactory appearance. If filler is used, overnight drying time (at least 12 hours) should be allowed before applying the shellac. Filler under shellac is not recommended for maple or pine floors.

On oak floors, (filler or unfilled) 2–3 coats (2-pound cut) are required. Three coats (2-pound cut) are preferred for maple, as well as for pine and other soft woods. Allow first coat to harden 3 hours before second coat is applied. The first coat should be lightly hand-sanded before the application of the second coat. Allow the second coat at least overnight drying time before applying third coat.

VARNISH—Like shellac, varnish is available at wide ranges of price and quality. Cheap varnishes are usually poor in quality and tend to become brittle, powder, or show white scars. Although varnish is often considered more attractive than shellac, its extreme slow-drying has created a relative preference for faster-drying shellac for floor finishing. So-called "quick dry" varnishes are often less durable than standard varnishes. Both all-purpose varnishes and varnishes for floors or other specific uses are available.

Since the average acceptable floor varnish requires at least 24 hours to dry, it is necessary to protect the newly varnished surface from dust, lint, insects, etc., during this drying period, at least until the finish becomes tac-free (4–8 hours). On oak floors, the use of a filler is preferred prior to the application of the first coat of varnish. The filler should dry at least 12 hours before varnishing. For most floors, 3 coats of varnish are recommended.

Most varnishes are packaged ready to apply and, when reduction is required, turpentine is ordinarily used. Both the first and second coats should be hand-sanded when dry. All coats require a 24 hour drying period at normal temperature and humidity.

Although varnish outranks shellac in water resistance, it is nevertheless susceptible to scratching and marking and becomes progressively darker with age. Varnish is characteristically a softer finish and in time dirt and grime may unduly harm the finish resulting in unsightly floor areas. For cleaning varnished floors, soap should be used sparingly and, when used, should be thoroughly removed. Periodic waxing reduces the time and effort otherwise required to keep varnished floors clean and attractive.

SEALERS—Unlike shellac and varnish, both of which are surface coatings, most floor seals are formulated to penetrate into the wood and harden at the surface to seal the floor against dirt, moisture, stains and other foreign materials. Although wood floors are thus sealed, the actual surface of the wood is exposed to the abrasive action of footsteps unless some surface protection is provided. For this reason, constant waxing of sealed floors is necessary. If regular waxing is neglected, the wood itself is exposed and, therefore, subject to premature wear.

Since one of its chief purposes is the sealing of floors, wood filler is rarely recommended under floor seals. If filler is used, the penetrative effect of the seal is so greatly reduced as to virtually become akin to a surface finish.

Most floor seals are applied with a brush or a lamb's-wool mop. The seal is applied liberally and the correct amount penetrates after about 15 to 20 minutes. Any surplus material remaining on the surface after that period should be removed with a dry cloth or mop. After 12 to 24 hours, depending upon drying conditions, the surface is buffed lightly with a power buffer, using fine steel wool; then the second coat of seal is applied. Before the second coat dries on the surface, any excess material should be removed as before. The second coat is allowed to dry thoroughly—about 24 hours—and the floor is again buffed with fine steel wool to obtain a hard, smooth-wearing surface.

Old Wood Floors

In refinishing a wood floor, it is necessary first to remove the old finish. Varnish or paint may be taken off by machine sanding and scraping or with the aid of a paint remover.

Commercial, non flammable, and organic-solvent type removers have instructions on the labels which should be carefully followed. The removers are usually applied to the floor with a brush and allowed to stand for a few minutes. In brushing, care should be taken not to damage the finish on baseboard and moldings. After the remover has been allowed to stand for the required time, the varnish or paint will soften so that it can be scraped off with a putty knife or rubbed off with excelsior or steel wool. If a putty knife is used, it should be held in a vertical position, scraping toward the operator across the grain of the wood so as not to splinter the flooring. The floor can then be washed several times with clear water and when thoroughly dry, may be sanded, dusted, and refinished the same as a new floor.

Spots or Stains

Wood floors that are spotted or discolored may be bleached with a solution prepared by dissolving 1 teaspoon of oxalic acid in half a pint of hot water. The solution should be applied to the floor, allowed to stand overnight, and removed by rinsing with clear water, after which the floor should be allowed to dry. When dry, the floor can be refinished by filling the cracks and holes with a commercial crack filler colored to match

the wood, applying sealer, and covering with wax, shellac, or varnish.

Painted Floors

For floors that are discolored and in poor condition, it may be more practical to cover the imperfections with two or three coats of porch and deck enamel than to refinish by other methods. The enamel may be applied to a floor from which all dirt, grease, and wax have been removed to produce an attractive, abrasive-resistant finish. The enamels are obtainable in many colors and may be applied as a solid color or to give a splatter-dash effect by using several colors. The manufacturer's directions should be followed concerning the thinning and the time allowed for drying between coats. After the last coat has thoroughly dried, it should be given two coats of solvent-thinner wax and buffed. A floor finished in this manner should be cleaned with a dry mop and the wax coating renewed frequently in the traffic area.

Maintenance

Waxed floors should be maintained by cleaning with a soft brush or mop free from oil since oil softens the wax. Volatile-solvent type floor waxes, as well as the dirt embedded therein, can be removed surface first with 00 steel wool dipped in turpentine or mineral spirits and then with a soft cloth. After this the floor may be refinished with several thin coats of wax, being sure that each coat is thoroughly dried and polished before applying the next coat.

Wax coatings of the water-emulsion type may be removed by scrubbing the surface with a warm solution of soap and water (about 120° to 130° F.), using a soft bristle brush or cloth. When the floor is clean, a thin coat of water—emulsion wax may again be applied, allowed to dry thoroughly, and buffed lightly.

Varnished and shellacked floors which are unwaxed should be dusted clean with a soft brush or dry mop and then rubbed with an oiled mop or a cloth slightly moistened with floor oil or furniture polish. In general, varnished and shellacked surfaces should not be treated with water. The appearance of badly worn varnished wood may be improved by coating with self-polishing floor wax.

Painted floors may be maintained by sweeping them with a soft brush and then rubbing them with an oiled mop or cloth. Occasionally they may be washed with slightly soapy water, rinsed with a wet cloth or mop, wiped dry, and then polished with an oiled cloth.

Floor Jack

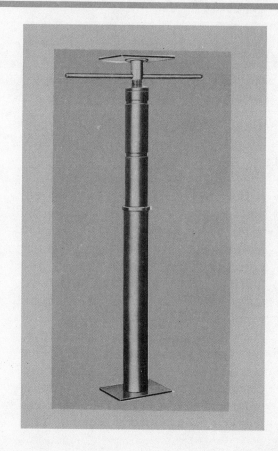

This is a specialized jack used to correct sagging floors. Usually adjustable in height, up to about 8', these metal columns can be used to raise a sagging floor gradually, or one may be used to raise the floor to the required level so that wood supports can be set under the floor.

Also see *FLOOR REPAIRS*.

A floor jack used to correct sagging wooden floors.

Floor Plan

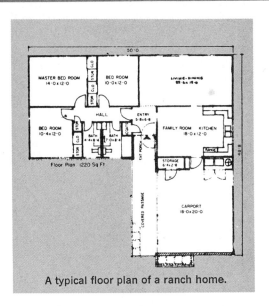

A typical floor plan of a ranch home.

An architectural drawing which shows the length and width of a building of the rooms, stairs, doors and windows and other features it contains. A separate plan is made for each level or floor.

Also see *HOUSE PLANS*.

Floor Repairs

The two most common types of floor construction used in residences are wood and concrete, finished or covered in various ways.

Wood Floors

Wood floors on joists usually consist of a subfloor, building paper and a finish flooring of hard or soft wood. In some cases, however, one layer of finish flooring may be applied directly to the joists without subflooring. In the course of time, wood floors may sag or develop cracks, and floor boards may become loose and creak when walked on. Floors may sag if the joists are too light for the length of span; sagging may also occur if there is shrinkage in the wood girder that supports the ends of the floor joists or if there is settling in the footings or foundations upon which the posts supporting the girder rest.

The amount of sag in joists can be determined by stretching a chalk line or string taut across the floor at right angles to the joists and tacking it to the surface of the floor on opposite sides of the room. If there is access to the space beneath the floor, such as a basement or excavated area, this sag can be corrected by the use of adjustable steel posts which operate as a screw jack to raise the sag in the joists until the surface of the finished floor is in line with the taut string.

These jack posts may be obtained from mail-order houses or hardware dealers at reasonable cost. One or more may be necessary. The bottom of each post should rest on a firm bearing such as the concrete floor in a basement or a concrete or masonry pedestal or base built on the ground in an excavated area. A stout plank or beam of sufficient

strength to carry the load and support the sagging joists should be placed on top of each post at right angles to the joists.

The steel post may be left in place permanently or may be used as a tool in installing a wood post. If a steel post is left in place, it should be located under the center of the sag. On the other hand, if a wood post is preferred as a permanent installation, the steel post or jack should be placed far enough off center to allow space for the wood post to be inserted. After the wood post has been installed and made secure with hardwood shims or wedges between the top of the post and the bottom of the beam, the steel post can be removed.

Cracks in a new floor are usually the result of shrinkage in floor boards which have not been properly seasoned or which have been exposed to excessive moisture before or during construction. Although it will not entirely conceal them, the cracks may be sealed with filler which will set hard and be durable. Wide cracks can be more effectively filled by gluing in narrow strips of wood, planed to fit tight.

Creaking Floors

Floors may creak when walked on for several reasons:

- If floor boards have not been properly laid,
- If they have not been properly nailed,
- If the floor boards or floor joists have become warped, or

Floor jack should be mounted with a wood block directly under the beam and immediately over the jack.

• If the floor construction as a whole is faulty.

Other causes for creaking floors are shrinkage and warping that result from the finish floor or the subfloor being damp when laid, warping that results from the finish floor being laid in the same direction as the subfloor, and warping that results from the finish floor being nailed directly to the joists, omitting the subfloor.

If the basement has no ceiling, the location and direction of joists under the first floor and whether the floor is single or double may be readily determined. In the case of the second-story floor, however, it is more difficult to be sure whether a floor is single or double. If the finished flooring on the second floor runs in the same direction as that on the first floor, it may be assumed that the same type of construction has been used for both floors.

The following tools and materials are needed: hammer, nail set, and block of wood; small quantities of 3d-finishing nails for $\frac{3}{8}''$ dressed and matched hardwood flooring, 8d cut flooring nails for $1\frac{3}{16}''$ or $1''$ common flooring, and 10d cut flooring nails for $1\frac{1}{16}''$ flooring.

The bridging of floor joists should be examined where exposed and strengthened or nailed securely at the points where creaking is evident. Floor boards that have become slightly raised from the joists may be forced back into position by laying a thick covering of old carpet or several-thicknesses of paper over the raised portion of the floor to protect the finish, placing a block of wood on top of the covering, and striking the block with a heavy ham-

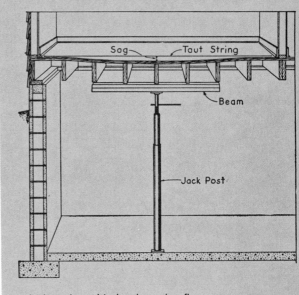

Jack post used to level sagging floors.

mer to drive the flooring back into place.

If this does not produce the desired results, a few nails may be driven around the loose area to draw the boards down tight. Resin-coated finishing or casing nails long enough to penetrate the subflooring and supporting joists should be used.

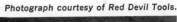

Photograph courtesy of Red Devil Tools.

Care should be taken not to bend the nails and, when the heads are within a quarter of an inch of the floor, a nail set should be used to drive the heads below the surface to prevent marring the floor with the hammer. The nail holes should then be filled with putty or wood filler and finished like the floor. If the top surface of the joists will not hold nails securely, it may be necessary to fasten blocking to the sides of the joists and drive the floor nails into the blocking.

If the methods described are not successful on the first floor, it may be supported and the creaking eliminated by driving a thin strip of wood between the bottom of the flooring and the top of the joists. Another method to stop creaking is to nail a cleat of wood to the side of the joists high enough to support the flooring. In extreme cases, it may be necessary to remove some of the finish flooring, nail the sub-flooring securely to the joists, and replace the finish flooring.

Concrete Floors

Concrete floors are usually finished with a smooth surface and ordinarily require little maintenance. If a concrete floor cracks deeply or the surface flakes excessively, little can be done except to refinish the floor with new material. A new concrete finish should be applied. See *CONCRETE*.

The surface of old concrete may be hardened somewhat to reduce dusting, although in the construction of a concrete floor hardening treatments are not a substitute for poor materials and shoddy workmanship.

Waterglass may be used to reduce dusting.

If colored pigments have been mixed in the concrete topping at time of laying, the surface may be treated with a penetrating varnish seal and a bright clean luster maintained by applying floor wax at intervals. Floor dyes or stains for concrete that will penetrate the surface to some extent are also available. They should be applied with a bristle brush, using a scrubbing motion. After these stains have been applied, the surface finish can be maintained with colored wax. The wax should be buffed with a floor polishing machine.

Two types of finishes may be used on concrete floors: enamels that have a varnish base, and rubber-base paints. Where the concrete floor is dry and does not rest on the ground, concrete floor enamels with a varnish base will give good service. Where the concrete floor rests on the ground and may be subject to dampness, rubber-base paints should be used. The floor must be clean and dry when either paint is applied. Paint films should be protected by floor wax.

Flower Boxes and Planters

For growing plants in the house or on the window sill, you may devise simple boxes or larger planters which add to the decorative theme as well as prove their usefulness for the "green thumb" householder.

Tropical Plants—Wardian Case

A planter enclosed in glass is recommended here, as tropical plants may not thrive well in a heated room where the atmosphere may be too dry. This holds true for other varieties of plants which need a high humidity. For such condition, the Wardian case is suggested.

This may be a single flower pot placed under a glass bell or an inverted fish bowl, or it may be a box which you build with glass sides and top. Place at the bottom of the single pot or the box, containers of damp moss which keep the inside of the case moist.

For a more decorative object, you could build this case to stand on legs, with two or more shelves on which you place the small individual pots of flowers; have the top, back, and two sides of glass stationary, with the glass front on a hinge to be raised when necessary. Under the bottom shelf you could place the containers of moist moss to sustain the humidity needed. As a further decorative note, you could make the shelves in step formation, the top ones narrower than the bottom. This is especially effective with small, tropical plants in colorful individual pots.

Indoor Window Box

The principle of the Pennsylvania Dutch sink is a good idea to follow

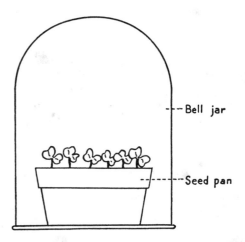

here, as it gives a sunken area in which to place the flower pots, as well as a cupboard underneath for storing the watering can, extra pots, and other paraphernalia which the indoor gardener uses.

You can buy one of these sink-cupboards, or build one yourself, and install it under a window. The recessed top should be lined with zinc, lead, aluminum, or sheet copper, and the corners soldered so water will not leak out. If you make this planter-cupboard yourself, you could use plywood for the cupboard part of it, and make either a single or double door; of course, provide whatever shelves inside the cupboard section that you will need.

However, if you do not want the cupboard, you could build this planter on four legs, and then make it secure under the window to enable it to bear the weight of the plants. Here, too, build the top in the form of a sink, and line it with metal.

When painted the color of the wall, this planter produces a charming addition to the room decoration as well as being a good way of harboring the indoor plants.

Window Sill Box

You may buy this ready-made, or make it yourself. The box may be installed on the window sill, or perhaps around the floor or extension rail of a porch. There are many considerations to the purchase or making of a box. It should be roomy, with enough depth and height. Avoid a metal box because metal may heat up in the sun and prove harmful by drying out the soil and the plants.

Wood should be well seasoned and of a kind to bear up under weather conditions. Of course, you might want to carry out the exterior style of the house in the flower boxes by having them made of tile, terra cotta, concrete, or whatever material is appropriate.

As some localities prohibit the installation of flower boxes outside the window, especially on a higher floor, it is best that you make certain before you do any constructing or installing.

For planting hints, it is a good idea to keep the flowers separately in pots, then place the pots into the box. In this manner, you can move the plants or make replacements as you desire. However, if you do the planting in the box directly, be sure to use a loose, rich soil and apply sufficient fertilizer. Don't fill the soil to the top of the box. Bore holes in the box or use whatever method you feel is most feasible to allow for drainage.

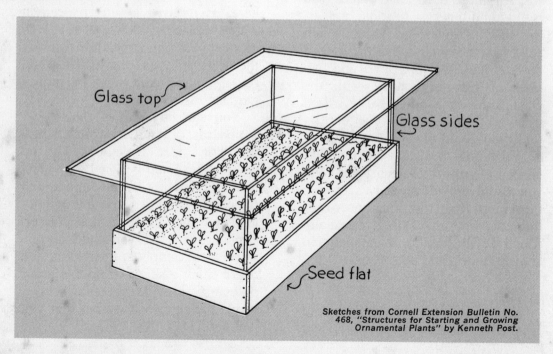

Sketches from Cornell Extension Bulletin No. 468, "Structures for Starting and Growing Ornamental Plants" by Kenneth Post.

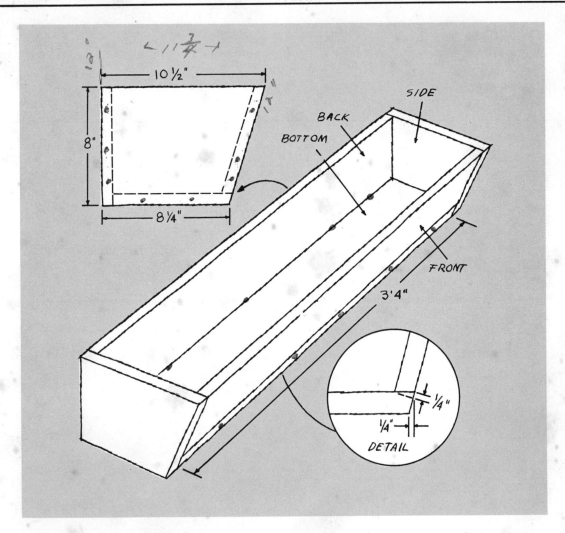

Constructing Window Box

As a suggestion for a wooden flower box, here is a plan and procedure. You will change this, of course, to suit the dimensions you have available. For the plan here you need 12′ of 1x8 board.

FRONT, BACK, AND BOTTOM

1. From a 1x8 board, 12′ long, cut three pieces each 3′ 4″ long, squaring their ends and marking them Front, Back, and Bottom.

2. Plane off a ¼″ level on one edge of the bottom piece and both edges of the front piece.

ENDS

1. Cut a piece of 1x8 board 2′ long (the piece left from the 12′ length) and square its edges.

2. Lay the piece flat, with the grain running right and left.

3. From the left end, measure to the right along the far edge of the board 10½″ and make a mark.

4. From the mark made in step 3 measure another 8½″ to the right, make a mark, and, with the aid of a square, draw a line across the width of the board at this point.

5. From the left end of the board, measure along the near edge 8½″ to

the right and make a mark.

6. Connect the points marked in steps 3 and 5 with a line.

7. Saw along the lines drawn in steps 4 and 6.

8. Place the two end pieces in a vise and true their edges so that both are the same.

ASSEMBLING THE PARTS

1. With four #8, 1½" flathead wood screws, fasten the bottom to the back piece and countersink the heads even with the surface.

2. With ten #8, 1½" flathead wood screws, fasten the ends to the back and bottom, being careful to keep all edges even.

3. With six #8, 1½" flathead wood screws, fasten the front piece in place.

FINISHING

Shellac any knots and thoroughly cover the box with a good quality paint of the color desired. It is well to paint the inside of the box with exterior paint to protect it.

The outside of the box may be painted to blend with the colors of the house.

Flowers, Cut

When you've cut some flowers from your garden to decorate your home, you may preserve them longer by following these hints.

Drop a lump of charcoal into the vase. This keeps the water odor-free and prevents rapid decay of the flowers.

Cut the stems of the flowers on a slant before setting them into the bowl or vase containing the water.

More water is absorbed by the stem when it has the slanted cut.

Chrysanthemums and other flowers with hard stems should be slit a few inches from the bottom of the stem, or else the base of the stems crushed, before being placed in water.

A vase sometimes topples over if it doesn't have a base that is steady enough to hold up the weight of the flowers. To prevent this top-heavy situation, put a few marbles or pebbles or a lead weight into the bottom of the vase.

Flue

See *CHIMNEY*.

Fluid Drive

This is a constant-torque drive mechanism which was built into the flywheel of the early 1940 automobiles. It consists of two discs or rotors which have fins or vanes and both are enclosed in a case with oil. As one of these discs or rotors revolves, it causes the oil within the unit to move and set up a reciprocating action on the part of the other rotor.

Slippage between the rotors or discs varies inversely to the speed. This permits a smooth start of a car in any gearshift position. Fluid drive rotors do not touch each other—there is always oil between them.

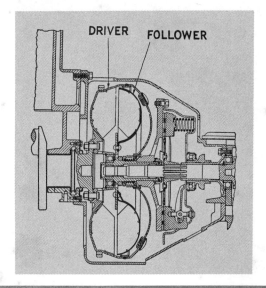

Cross-section of fluid drive mechanism showing position of driver and follower—the rotors with vanes.

Fluorescent Lights

Fluorescent lights were originally considered proper only for lighting in commercial buildings, but have now become part of house lighting, with some very interesting and attractive results. They are used in work areas in the kitchen, laundry, bathroom, and workshop; they are adaptable for indirect, recessed and cove lighting in the other rooms of the house.

The principle of fluorescent lighting is a long glass tube filled with gasses which glow when the electrical current passes through the tube. About two or three times more light is received per watt from a fluorescent lamp than from the usual bulb. There is less heat given off, and the glare is less than from the incandescent bulb.

For information or repairing, see *ELECTRICAL WIRING*.

Circular fluorescent light fixtures are frequently used in kitchens.

Flush Door Projects

It's easy to make fine furniture when you start with an attractive flush door. Maybe you have removed the door and replaced it with a fold-ing door. Or you can purchase a flush door and then start your project.

Here are several projects involving the use of a flush door. These are just a few ideas. If you think about it, you will probably come up with many more. For construction details, see section on *FURNITURE*.

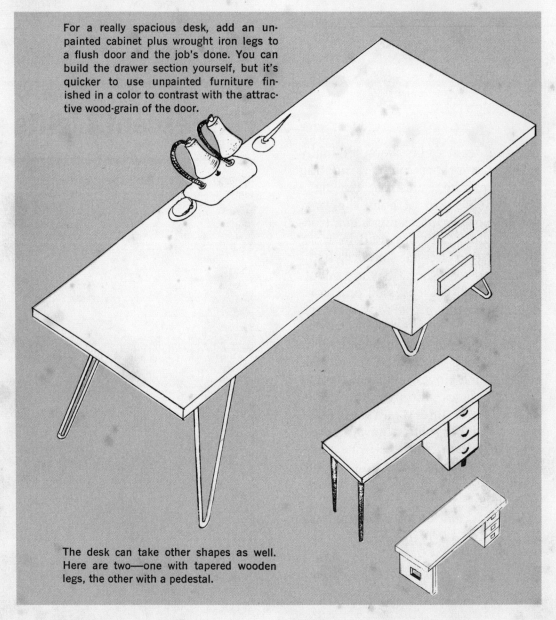

For a really spacious desk, add an un-painted cabinet plus wrought iron legs to a flush door and the job's done. You can build the drawer section yourself, but it's quicker to use unpainted furniture fin-ished in a color to contrast with the attrac-tive wood-grain of the door.

The desk can take other shapes as well. Here are two—one with tapered wooden legs, the other with a pedestal.

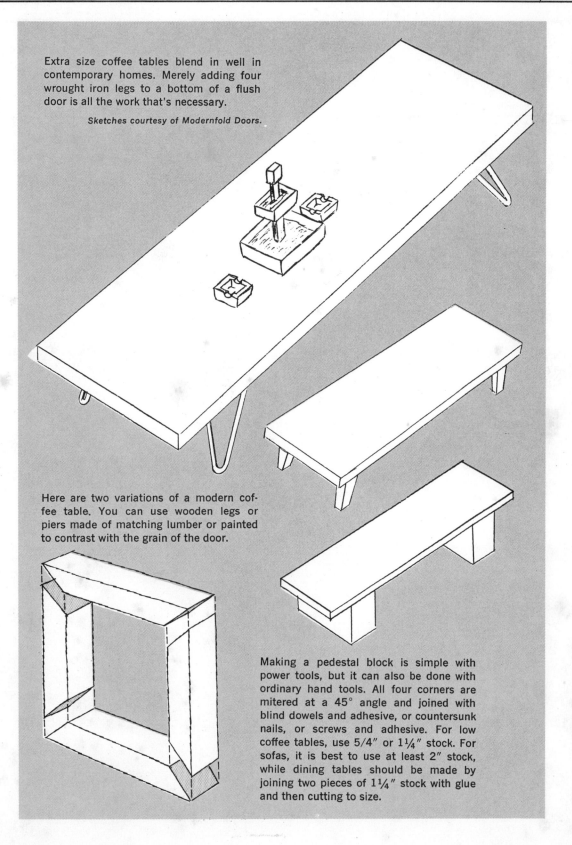

Extra size coffee tables blend in well in contemporary homes. Merely adding four wrought iron legs to a bottom of a flush door is all the work that's necessary.

Sketches courtesy of Modernfold Doors.

Here are two variations of a modern coffee table. You can use wooden legs or piers made of matching lumber or painted to contrast with the grain of the door.

Making a pedestal block is simple with power tools, but it can also be done with ordinary hand tools. All four corners are mitered at a 45° angle and joined with blind dowels and adhesive, or countersunk nails, or screws and adhesive. For low coffee tables, use 5/4" or $1\frac{1}{4}$" stock. For sofas, it is best to use at least 2" stock, while dining tables should be made by joining two pieces of $1\frac{1}{4}$" stock with glue and then cutting to size.

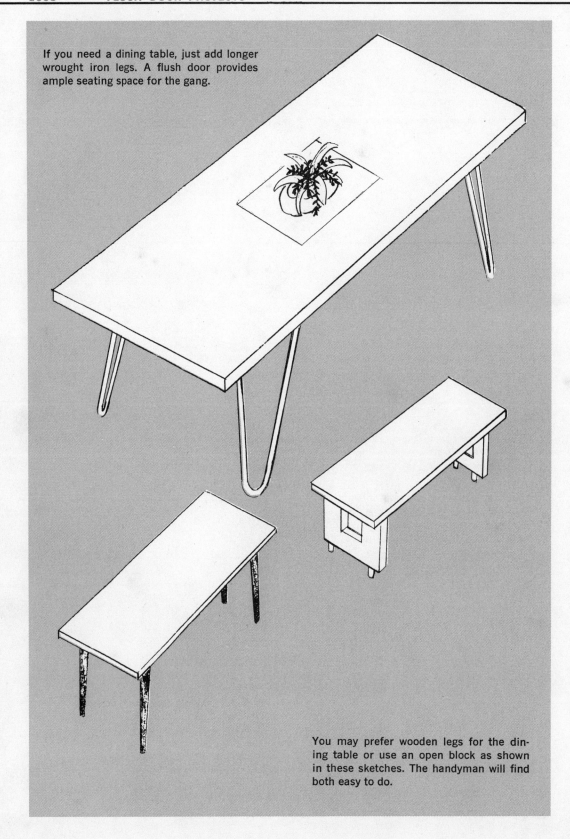

If you need a dining table, just add longer wrought iron legs. A flush door provides ample seating space for the gang.

You may prefer wooden legs for the dining table or use an open block as shown in these sketches. The handyman will find both easy to do.

Wrought iron legs, about 9″ high, plus a 4″ foam rubber mattress can be combined with a flush door to make an attractive sofa for the living room or game room. The handyman skilled with tools can cut out a section for a recessed planter, a decorative touch any homemaker will appreciate.

You can make sides for the sofa or not, as you please. Here are two variations, either of which is handy as an extra bed when company drops in.

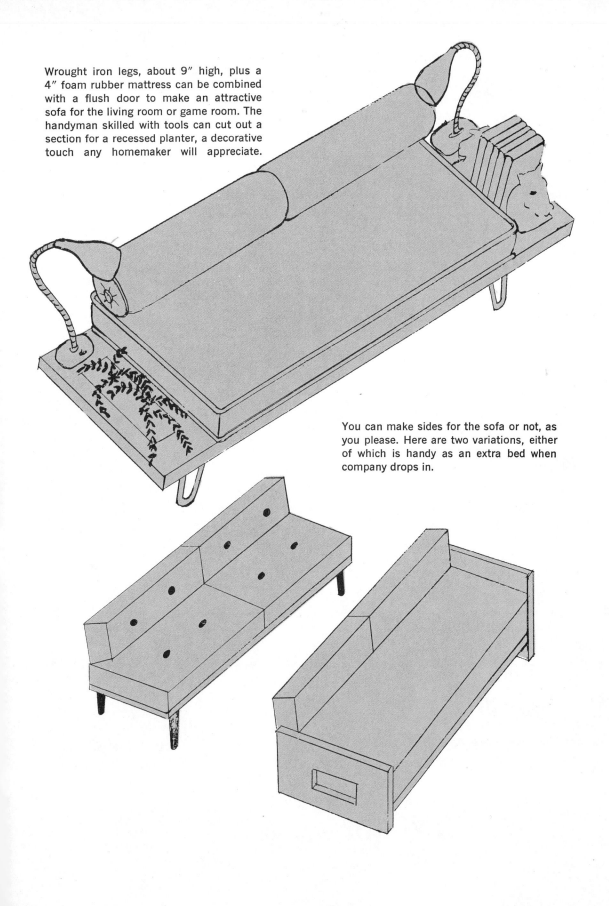

Flush Valve, Toilet

See *DRAINAGE SYSTEM*.

Fluxes

A flux is a chemical preparation (powder, paste, or liquid) used to keep metal clean so the solder will stick to it. If a flux is not used, the heat will cause oxides to form on the metal surface and prevent the solder from adhering firmly. The usual fluxes for common metals are:

METAL	FLUX
Brass, copper, tin	Rosin
Lead	Tallow, rosin
Iron, steel	Borax, sal-ammoniac
Galvanized iron	Zinc chloride
Zinc	Zinc chloride
Aluminum	Stearine, special flux

Fluxes are either corrosive or non-corrosive. The commonly used corrosive fluxes, zinc chloride and sal-ammoniac, eat away and corrode the metal if allowed to remain on it after soldering. They should be completely removed by a thorough washing after you've finished a job. It is for this reason that rosin, a non-corrosive flux is used when soldering electrical connections. The rosin is used in powdered form, or as a liquid core for wire solder.

Paste fluxes, commercially manufactured, are usually available in cans. They contain grease for counteracting corrosion, but this grease sticks to the metal and collects dirt. Paste fluxes are substitutes for the acid fluxes. They are safer to use and are particularly useful for odd-job soldering, or at times when it is inconvenient to mix and use zinc chloride.

For information on how to use flux when soldering, refer to the section on *SOLDERING*.

Foam Rubber

Have you a yen to "do over" a chair or some other piece of upholstered furniture in your home? It is much simpler and easier with latex foam. And the results will amaze you —more beauty, more comfort, and a cushioning material that will never wear out. Here's how to do it:

Equipment You Will Need

No complicated special equipment is needed for upholstering with latex foam. It can be cut, shaped or

trimmed with regular shears, a sharp knife, or razor. The only other items you will need for working are rubber fabricating cement, ordinary tacking tape (or special latex foam adhesive tape), and soapstone.

Marking Your Pattern

Patterns may be marked on latex foam with a soft lead or wax pencil, with talc dusted through a perforated pattern, or with talc dusted around the edges of a solid pattern.

Cutting

Latex foam can be cut to any desired shape quickly and easily. In general, add ¼" to your pattern on all sides (including arm and frame posts) for upholstering allowance.

Mounting

Over springs—use a suitable insulating pad (burlap, jute, cotton, sisal, etc.) to protect the latex foam cushioning from unnecessary rubbing or wear.

Over hard surfaces—apply latex foam directly on the base and secure it with tacking tape around the edges or by cementing it to the base. In the case of plywood, the base should be ventilated, if possible, with very small holes to permit free passage of air through the latex foam. Metal bases should have a rust-resistant finish.

Over webbing—apply latex foam directly over webbing (spaced for good ventilation) and secure with tacking tape around the edges.

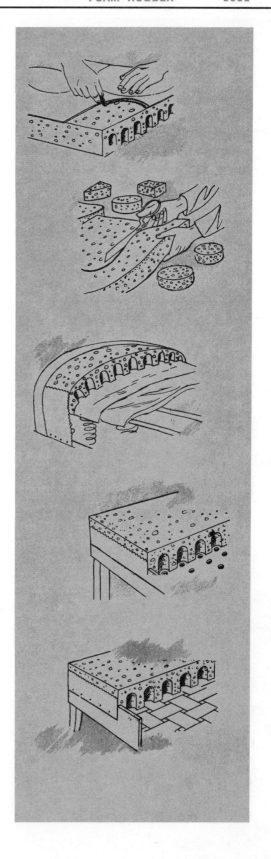

Using Tacking Tape

Tacking tape serves as an aid to edging, as a means of securing the cushion to the base, and as a handy reinforcement for holding a sharply defined edge. It can be fastened securely to the foam with rubber cement. Regardless of width, tape for tacking should be cemented on the foam about 1″ from the edge of the cushion. Frequently, tape is cemented to the edge of a reversible cushion and then sewed into the welt of the cushion cover to prevent slipping of the fabric.

How To Use Cement

Cement may be used for securing the latex foam padding and cushion to the base of frame, for fastening tacking tape and for joining sections and fabricating cushions. Cement should be applied to both sections to be joined and should be allowed to dry long enough to become "tacky" before pressing together. Any cement left exposed on surface after fabricating should be dusted with soapstone. Cemented pieces should be permitted to set for several hours before they are used.

How To Make Reversible Cushions

Reversible cushions may be made from slab stock in one of two ways:

(a) Using two pieces of cored utility stock, bevel all four edges on the cored side and cement together, smooth side out.

(b) Between two pieces of cored utility stock, place a smaller piece of 1″ cored utility stock or plain sheet stock and cement together. The cushion may be finished with square or rolled edges made from plain sheet stock.

Edging

You can make any type of edge you desire very simply, using either cored utility stock or plain sheet stock.

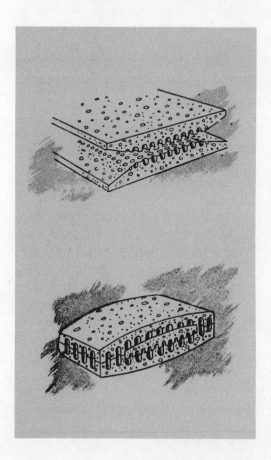

(a) Feathered Edge—Cut stock to proper cushion size, adding the usual ¼" all around for upholstering allowance. Cement tacking tape to cushion 1" from edge. Then bevel lower edge to the necessary degree for the desired contour. Draw tape down so that the beveled edge of the cushion is flat against the base and tack in place.

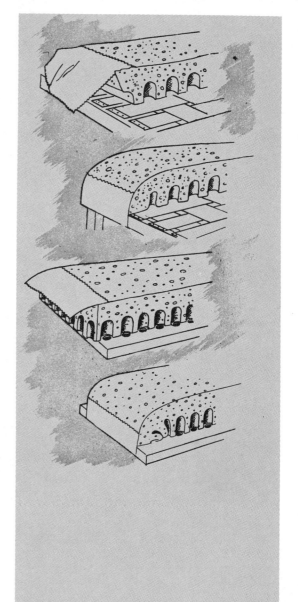

(b) Cushioned edge—Cut stock to cushion shape, adding the usual ¼" all around for upholstering allowance plus ½" for edge (total of ¾" over base measurement at cushion edge). Cement tape to foam 1" from edge. Tuck bottom edge of cushion under so that edge is flat against base, taking care to keep tape taut so foam does not wrinkle or bunch unevenly. Finally, tack tape to base.

(c) Square edges—For square edges of different types, cut stock to desired shape and size, adding the usual ¼" upholstering allowance all around. Cement tape flat against vertical edge and tack overhang to the base.

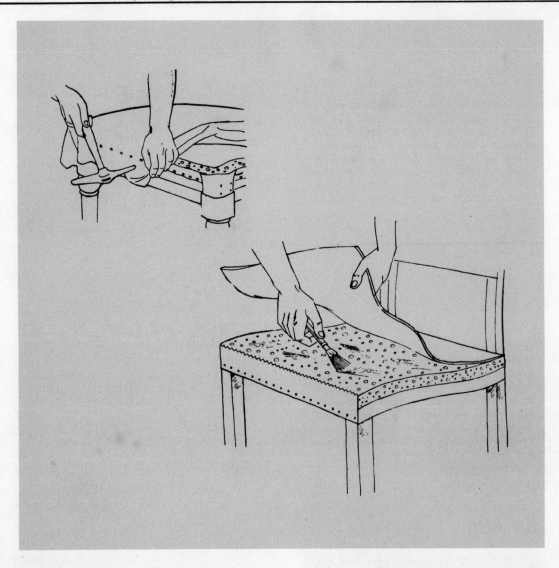

How To Cover Latex Foam

Material which has a tendency to stretch excessively should be avoided. When using extremely slippery, very loosely woven or high-pile fabrics, it is generally advisable to cover the foam first with muslin. Where leather, coated fabrics or plastic materials are desired, the supplier of the material should be consulted. He can recommend the proper material for use with latex foam.

Covers should be cut to fit neatly but not too tightly. As opposed to conventional upholstering materials, latex foam never packs down, so no allowance need be made for that. Also, covers should not be so tight as to compress the latex foam excessively, as too much cover tension reduces the depth of the cushion and detracts from the resilient comfort of the latex foam. When covering shaped seats it is often advisable to cement fabric lightly to the latex foam padding to keep the cover in position.

Also see *UPHOLSTERY*.

1. Make paper pattern or use the headboard for tracing outline, adding ½" on all sides.

A Padded Headboard

Here's an easy-to-do upholstering job which will give any bedroom that "decorator look." Begin by having the man of the house, or your local lumber company, cut a plywood headboard to the desired size and shape.

Photographs courtesy of The Natural Rubber Bureau.

2. Cut out and bevel top and sides on lower surface.

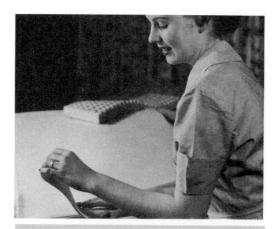

3. Apply tape on all four sides.

4. Smooth cushioned edges under carefully and tack in place.

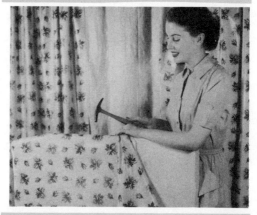

5. Finally, cover with the fabric you have chosen.

Folded Horn

This type of radio or phonograph speaker enclosure is capable of producing better bass at higher efficiency than any other type of speaker. It reduces distortion and eliminates or minimizes the resonant effects of the loudspeaker.

However, unless the folded horn is build in a precise manner, it will not fulfill its purpose. The average handyman without power tools should make a bass reflex cabinet. This unit is easier to make and requires less precise compound angle cutting.

For the advanced handyman and Hi-Fi enthusiast, here are plans for a University 3-Way Speaker System. All basic parts should be made out of

¾″ plywood and all joints held together with glue and screws. Furthermore, cleats, held by glue and screws, should be used to reinforce most of the joints as shown in the sketches.

Also see *HI-FI*.

View of folded horn with front grille cloth removed; note position of tweeter and two speakers.

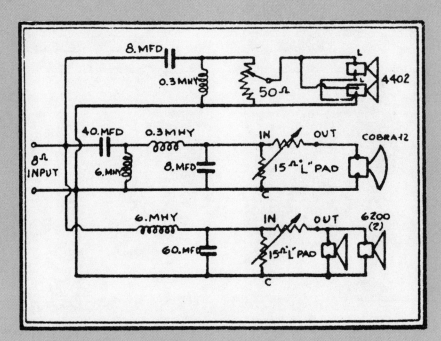

Schematic wiring diagram showing the speaker crossover network.

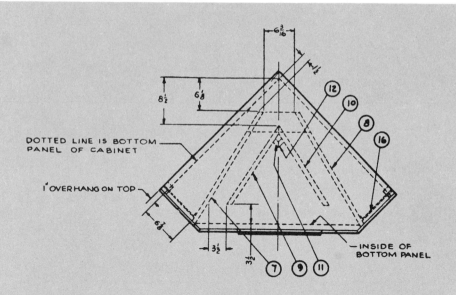

DOTTED LINE IS BOTTOM
PANEL OF CABINET

1" OVERHANG ON TOP

INSIDE OF
BOTTOM PANEL

Detailed view of the parts of the folded horn.

Sketches courtesy of University Speakers, Inc.

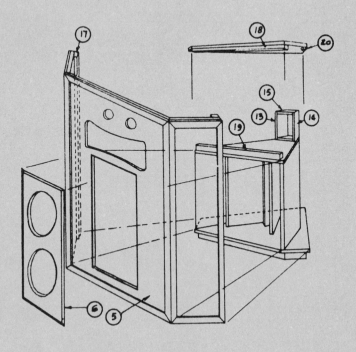

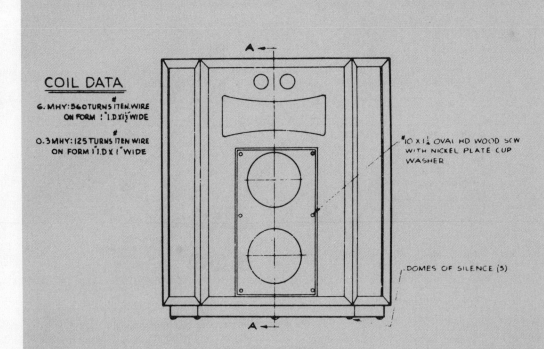

COIL DATA

6. MHY: 560 TURNS 17 EN. WIRE
ON FORM 1" I.D. X 1½" WIDE

0.3 MHY: 125 TURNS 17 EN WIRE
ON FORM 1" I.D. X 1" WIDE

#10 X 1¼ OVAL HD WOOD SCW
WITH NICKEL PLATE CUP
WASHER

DOMES OF SILENCE (5)

Front view of the unit showing exact location of the cut-outs for the speakers.

Sketches courtesy of University Speakers, Inc.

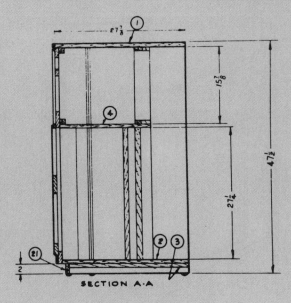

SECTION A·A

Cross section view through the center of the unit. Parts are numbered to correspond to the previous drawings.

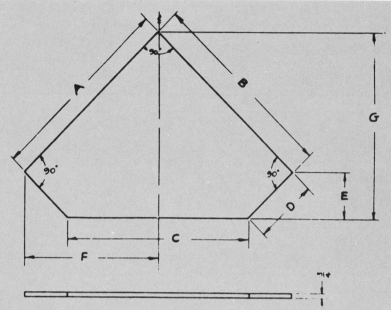

Basic measurements for top panel, bottom panel and bottom support.

PART	A—B	C	D	E	F	G
		(in inches)				
1. Top panel	29½	28	9¹³⁄₁₆	6⅞	21	27¾
2. Bottom panel	28⅝	29⅝	7¾	5⅜	14¹³⁄₁₆	25¾
3. Bottom support	23⅞	26	5⅜	4⅛	13	20⅞

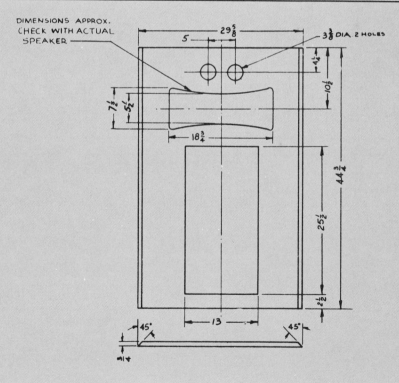

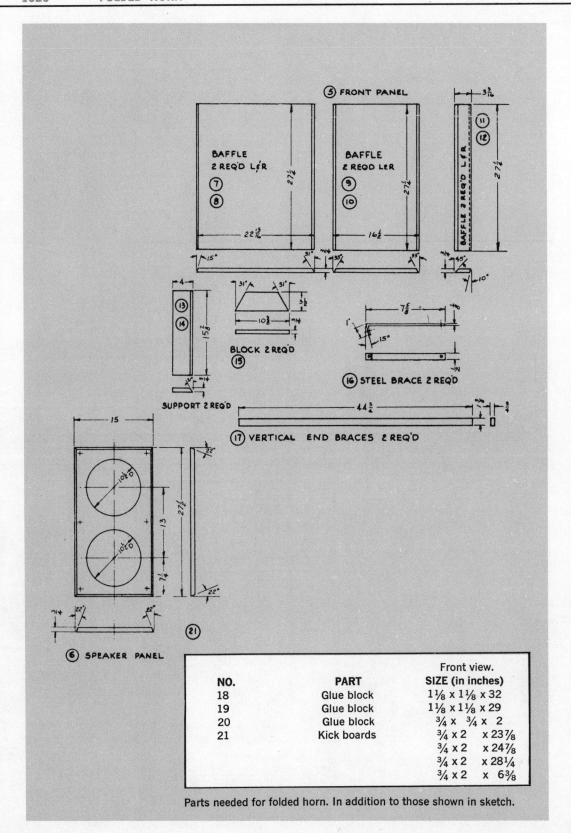

Parts needed for folded horn. In addition to those shown in sketch.

NO.	PART	Front view. SIZE (in inches)
18	Glue block	$1\frac{1}{8}$ x $1\frac{1}{8}$ x 32
19	Glue block	$1\frac{1}{8}$ x $1\frac{1}{8}$ x 29
20	Glue block	$\frac{3}{4}$ x $\frac{3}{4}$ x 2
21	Kick boards	$\frac{3}{4}$ x 2 x $23\frac{7}{8}$
		$\frac{3}{4}$ x 2 x $24\frac{7}{8}$
		$\frac{3}{4}$ x 2 x $28\frac{1}{4}$
		$\frac{3}{4}$ x 2 x $6\frac{3}{8}$

Folding Rule

Any ruler that can be collapsed is called a folding rule. Among professionals, there is only one folding rule. The other type, frequently called folding rules by the layman, are really zig-zag rules. A folding rule is convenient because it can be stored in the workshop or carried on the job and still occupy only a limited space.

Also see *MEASURING DEVICES*.

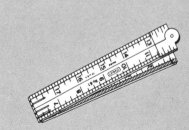

A folding rule is used mainly by the craftsman and professional.

Zig-zag rules are sometimes called folding rules. In about a 6" length, you have a rule which will open up to 6' or more. It's compact and convenient for storing and for carrying on the job.

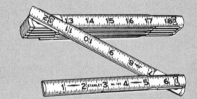

Sketch from "Tool Guide" courtesy of Stanley Tools.

Some zig-zag rules are made with extensions. A center slide slips out and makes measuring within a confined opening easier.

Footing

A term frequently misused as a synonym for foundation. It is a concrete or other masonry base under a wall, column, post or pier.

Also see *FOUNDATION*.

Fore Plane

This is an intermediate size plane. It is usually 18″ long with a 2⅜″ cutter or blade. It is used for finishing long edges or large surfaces.

A fore plane, 18″ long, is used primarily for finishing large wood surfaces.

Forstner Bit

This is a specialized centerless wood bit which comes in sizes from ¼″ up by ¹⁄₁₆″.

This type of bit is used to bore holes part of the way through the wood. It is used in place of the standard auger bit since the auger bit screw or spur would go through the wood.

The Forstner bit is also used on end grain, for boring holes in thin wood or near the end of a piece of wood where an auger bit might split the work.

It is possible to drill part of a hole along an edge of a board with a Forstner bit since no center boring hole is necessary.

To start a Forstner bit, scribe a circle the size of the hole with a pair of dividers and then press the rim of the bit into it. Once the outline has been set, you can proceed to bore the hole.

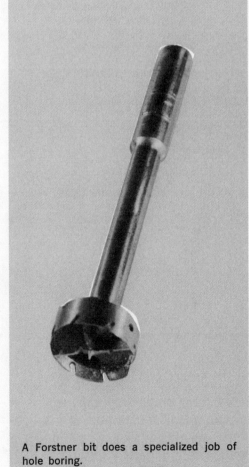

A Forstner bit does a specialized job of hole boring.

Foundation

All structures require a foundation which is secure enough to keep the walls and roof permanently in place. The foundation can be made of poured concrete, concrete or cinder blocks and other masonry materials. In some areas, concrete blocks can be used only if the voids or holes in the blocks are filled with concrete.

The foundation of a house generally extends several feet below ground level. If there is a basement, entire walls are used for the foundation. However, in houses built on piers, individual foundations are poured or built under each pier. In a slab house, a foundation is used along the perimeter.

The base of the foundation is called a footing. This footing, usually made of poured concrete, should be at least twice as wide as the foundation thickness. The footing is laid below the frost line and the foundation built above the footing.

It is essential that the foundation be constructed soundly so that the rest of the structure remains secure and stable. A shifting foundation or one with bad cracks can cause the upper structure to weaken. Therefore, follow local building code requirements related to the thickness and depth of the foundation before building any structure like a garage or an additional wing onto your home.

How To Build a Watertight Concrete Masonry Foundation

Recent construction trends in houses and farm buildings show that approximately two-thirds of the surface area of all masonry walls being built today in these fields use concrete block. This growth is largely due to the fact that concrete masonry is one of the most versatile, economical and durable all-purpose building materials known today.

In most sections of the United States and throughout Canada the big majority of homeowners want a basement—and they want it watertight. Many a homeowner has found it costs far more to repair a leaky basement than it does to build it watertight in the first place.

There's nothing difficult about building a watertight wall constructed of concrete masonry. These building units have, in general, been widely accepted as one of the recommended types of construction. Proper care in design and construction will assure a watertight concrete masonry basement wall.

Importance of Footings

The degree of watertightness is vitally dependent upon properly constructed footings. To make sure that uneven settlement won't cause cracks and leaks in the walls, concrete footings should be built of sufficient width and proportion to carry the load. General practice for residential construction requires footings to have a thickness equal to that of the foundation wall, and a width equal to twice the wall thickness. No parts of the footings should bear on freshly filled ground. It is also extremely im-

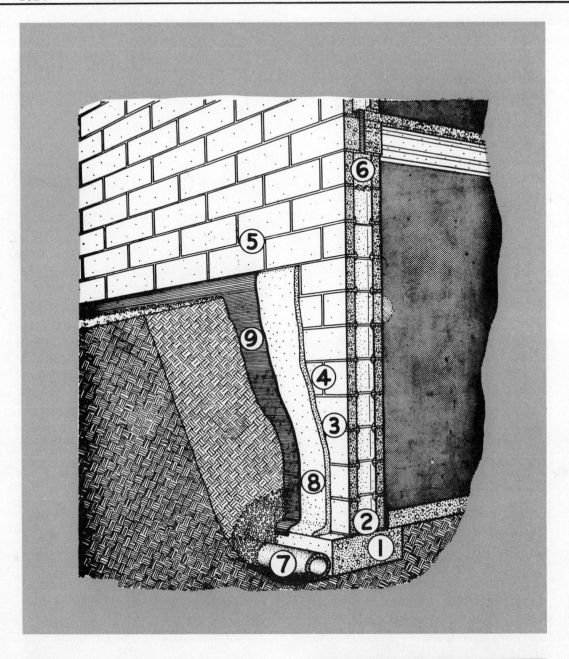

portant that downspouts be connected to underground drains, and that surface water be carried away by proper grading or by use of a sloping concrete gutter.

Unless construction is in a section of the country having a dry climate or the excavation is made in exceptionally well-drained subsoil, a line

This cut-away sectional drawing of a typical concrete masonry basement wall, complete with footings and drain tile.

of 4″ or 5″ drain tile should be placed entirely around the building at the footing level. The tile should have a slope of ½″ in 12′, and should

Build cast-in-place concrete footings at least 16″ wide and 8″ thick. Make sure they are carried to soil below the frost line.

Photographs courtesy of Portland Cement Association.

drain to a suitable outlet. Downspouts should not be connected to this tile. A sloping shoulder of mortar placed on the shelf formed by the footing will prevent water from collecting there. Joints between the tile can be covered with roofing felt to prevent sediment from filling the tile during backfilling. The tile should then be covered with 12″ to 18″ of coarse gravel or crushed stone to permit quick drainage.

TYPES OF MORTAR BEDDING—Two types of mortar bedding are common with concrete masonry—full mortar bedding and faceshell bedding. In full mortar bedding, the webs and face shells are covered and bedded in mortar. A full bed for mortar is used in laying the first or starting course of block on a footing or foundation wall. For all other concrete masonry work (with the exception of certain types of above-ground construction), the accepted practice is to use face-shell bedding.

In vertical joints, mortar is applied

only on the face shells of the units. After careful "buttering" of the vertical edges, each unit as placed is shoved against the block previously laid to produce well-compacted vertical mortar joints having good appearance.

Mortar should not be spread so far ahead of actual laying of units that it will tend to stiffen and lose its workability, resulting in a poor bond. Pressing the mortar against the units with a jointing tool after the mortar in the horizontal and vertical joints has stiffened somewhat is a big help in making a weathertight wall. A jointing tool compacts and presses the mortar firmly against the block, sealing the wall against moisture.

The first course of masonry should be placed on the concrete footing by using a full bed of mortar. Succeeding courses are laid by using face-shell bedding on vertical and horizontal face shells. The joints should be ⅜" thick and firmly compacted.

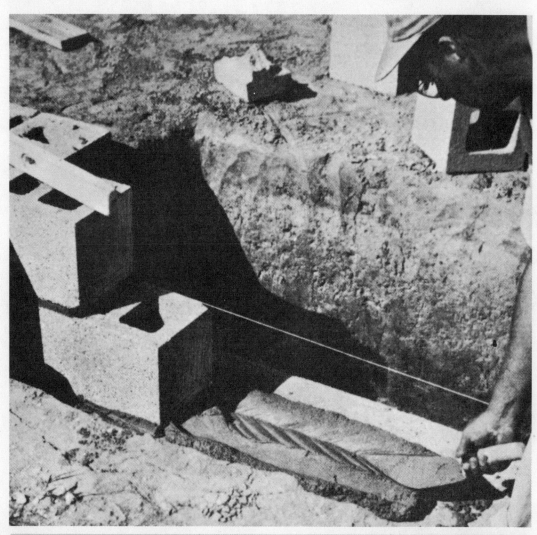

Using mortar of good quality, place a full bed on the center of the footing prior to laying the first course of concrete block.

Lay succeeding courses of concrete block plumb and level, using horizontal and vertical face shell bedding as pictured.

As an additional assurance of dry basement walls, two ¼" thick coats of plaster should be applied to all wall surfaces which will come in contact with the earth. These two coats of plaster should extend from 6" above the finished ground line down to the footing. The recommended mix for this plaster is in the proportions of 1 part of Portland cement to 2½ parts of damp, loose mortar sand. No hydrated lime is required in the plaster mix for coating concrete masonry basement walls.

The wall surface should be dampened prior to the application of the first coat of plaster. After the first coat has partially set, it should be roughened to provide good bond for the second coat and allowed to harden for at least 24 hours the second coat is applied. The first coat should be kept damp for at least 24 hours.

In poorly drained soil, after the plaster coats have hardened, the exterior surface of the basement wall can be given two continuous coatings of hot bituminous material applied at right angles to one another (over a suitable priming coat) and extending from 6" above the ground line down

Apply mortar to vertical face shells of one end of next block to be laid in the wall and then press the block firmly into position.

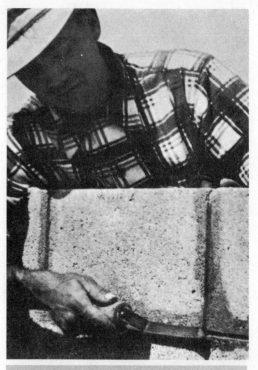

Since the wall is only as strong and as watertight as the mortar joints, compact all mortar joints with a jointing tool.

Use a solid top concrete block or fill the cores with concrete in the last course in the wall that will support floor slab or joists.

Except in dry climate or well-drained soil, lay drain tile around outside of footing and cover with 12″ to 18″ of coarse gravel.

Apply two ¼″ coats of Portland cement plaster to earth side of wall from 6″ above ground line down to the footing.

Photographs courtesy of Portland Cement Association.

over the top of the footing. The wall surface must be dry before the bituminous material is put on.

No filling against the concrete masonry basement walls should be permitted until the first floor is in place. Such precautions are necessary to insure sufficient bracing for the wall against lateral earth pressure.

Concrete masonry is economical to use because the units are relatively large, true to size and shape and can be laid in the wall faster and more efficiently than many other masonry materials. It isn't subject to destructive weathering or termites and, when given adequate foundation, concrete masonry basement walls stay as they were originally built. Patching and repairing is seldom, if ever, necessary.

Brush two coats of hot bituminous material over plaster. Brace wall and connect drain tile to outlet before back-filling.

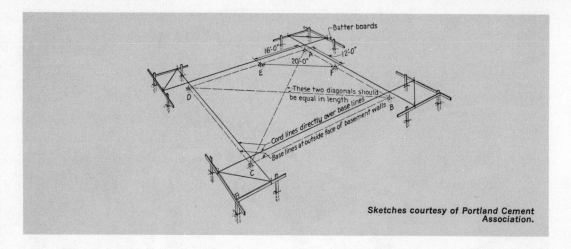

Sketches courtesy of Portland Cement Association.

Laying Out a Foundation

This is the right triangle method for laying out the foundation without use of surveying instruments.

1. Lay out a line representing outside face of basement wall, observing any requirements of local ordinances.
2. Set stakes at A and B on this line, locating two front corners.
3. Use nails in tops of all stakes for accurate location of all corners and other points.
4. Set stake F on line A-B 12′ from A.
5. Stake E is placed 16′ from A and 20′ from F. Angle EAB is a right angle.
6. Extend A-E to D for third corner of basement.
7. Locate C by an intersection of an arc described from D having a radius equal to A-B and an arc described from B having a radius equal to A-D.
8. To check accuracy of layout, A-C must equal B-D.
9. Set up batter boards outside limits of excavation.
10. Tops of all batter boards are set at same elevation, such as first-floor level.
11. Stretch heavy cord tightly between batter boards directly over base lines, thus establishing the building lines.

Here's how to set elevations of batter boards without surveying instruments.

1. Set batter boards at one corner as in sketch.
2. Place hose as shown.
3. Fill with water until water level is at top of batter board A.
4. Mark water level at opposite end B and set board to mark.

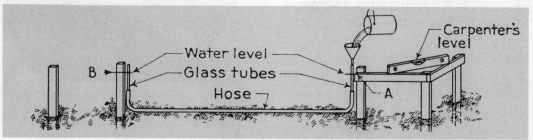

Foundation Planting

To enable you to design and choose the planting which is the foundation of your house exterior, refer to the section on *LANDSCAPING*.

Foundation Walls—Cracks

Cracks or fissures in foundation walls and falling mortar between joints may be attributed to various causes. Cracks between mortar and the material to which it was originally bonded may be caused by shrinkage of the mortar during setting, or soon thereafter, or by the expansion of mortar through saturation. Often the volume change of the mortar is greater than the material to which it is bonded and this change sets up a movement that destroys the bond.

If the walls are built on ground that will not support an equal weight at all points, uneven settling may cause cracks to develop. An underground spring of flowing water under one corner or section of a foundation may produce similar results. Small cracks thus started may become larger in time from action of the weather and other forces. Frost has a tendency to attack weak spots. Expansion and contraction caused by extremes of heat and cold increase the damage, and water seeping through the cracks gradually wears away the material, causing it to crumble and fall apart. The disintegration is generally more rapid in mortar joints.

Results of such disintegration are far reaching and if not remedied may cause further damage not only to the walls themselves but to the structure they support. A basement will probably become damp and unsanitary if these inlets for moisture are not closed.

Extent of Damage

If the walls are otherwise in good condition, minor cracks and places

To repair a crack in the outside of the foundation wall, brush away the debris and soak the area thoroughly.

where mortar has fallen out may be repaired by an unskilled workman. If, however, a wall is badly cracked and crumbled beyond the aid of minor repairs, it may be necessary to engage an experienced workman to reconstruct all or part of the wall.

Minor repairs require the following tools and materials; hammer, sharp-edged and pointed instrument (such as a cold chisel or screw driver), wire brush or whisk broom, small mixing board, mason's trowel and water bucket; Portland cement, a finely divided material such as hydrated lime, clean sand, and water.

Preparing Old Surfaces

Loose mortar between masonry courses should be chipped and picked out, and the joint brushed thoroughly to remove all dust and loose particles. The cleaned surface should be dampened before new mortar is applied to prevent absorption of water from the mixture.

Mortar

To make repairs, a mixture of 1 part Portland cement to 2½ parts sand, or 1 part cement to 3 parts sand, is recommended in ordinary cases. However, a 1:2 mixture is recommended for damp basements or those exposed to very moist conditions. A 1:2 mixture represents 1 part of Portland cement to 2 parts of sand, measured by volume. The proportion to be used will depend entirely upon conditions, a larger proportion of cement being necessary in cases where excessive moisture prevails.

Enough water should be used to make a fairly dry mortar about the

Use some ready-mixed cement or prepare a mix of one part of Portland cement to 2½ parts of sand; then add water.

Trowel on the cement mix over the crack, forcing it into the opening.

consistency of putty. The mortar should be thoroughly mixed and worked to insure best results. In filling cracks, the mortar should be applied like a calking material, that is, well rammed and tamped in to form contact with all corners and depressions to make a complete bond. When the crack has been tightly packed, the surface should be smoothed off with a trowel. In pointing up joints in masonry, the mortar may be applied with a trowel, and the surface finished to conform with the old mortar.

After the material has hardened, the new work should be kept wet for several days to increase the strength of the mortar. If work has been done on the outside of walls, they should be covered by tarpaulins to protect them from direct exposure to the sun and drying winds.

Foundation and Basement Drainage

Damp Basements

If the basement is damp, the difficulty may be traced to penetration of moisture through the walls and floor because of improper subdrainage. More often, however, the damp condition is due to condensation of moisture on chilled wall surfaces.

Flooding is usually caused by defective walls, lack of drain tile, careless backfilling, or improper grading around the wall, allowing surface water to pass into the basement. The condition of the walls themselves should be examined in order to detect cracks or loose mortar and repairs should be made.

Diverting Surface Water

Because wet basements often result from water penetrating the walls or floors, this water should be carried off before it comes in contact with the foundation. Water from roofs should be carried away by adequate gutters, conductors, and downspouts. The downspouts should be connected to a drain emptying into a storm sewer, dry well, open water course, or other suitable outlet. Many communities prohibit the draining of surface water into sanitary sewers. Where downspouts are not connected to an outlet, it is advisable to place a spatter board or splash block of good size at the outlet to divert the roof water away from the wall.

Quick shedding of water is essential and in many cases this may be accomplished by proper grading. The usual method is to place additional filling against the basement wall and grade it down to a sharp, smooth slope that extends at least 8' or 10' from the wall. The slope should be sown with good grass seed or sodded,

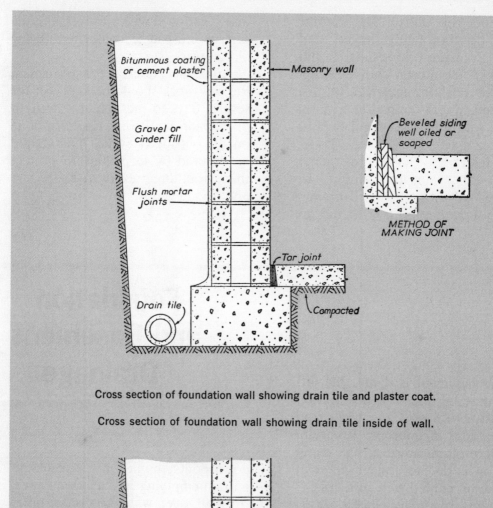

Bituminous coating or cement plaster

Masonry wall

Gravel or cinder fill

Flush mortar joints

Beveled siding well oiled or soaped

METHOD OF MAKING JOINT

Tar joint

Drain tile

Compacted

Cross section of foundation wall showing drain tile and plaster coat.

Cross section of foundation wall showing drain tile inside of wall.

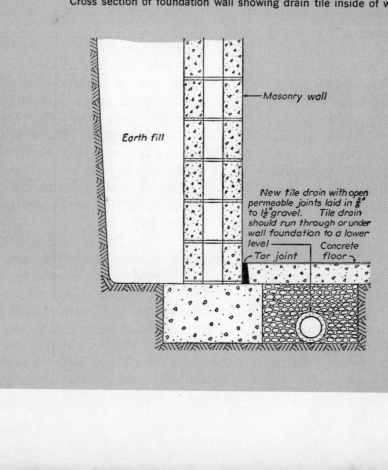

Masonry wall

Earth fill

New tile drain with open permeable joints laid in 3/4" to 1 1/2" gravel. Tile drain should run through or under wall foundation to a lower level

Concrete floor

Tar joint

and then rolled firmly and evenly. If necessary to grade above the basement window sills, a curved or rectangular area wall of concrete, brick, or metal should be built around them. Hinged covers for closing the openings during heavy rains or snow may also be provided. In any case, it is advisable to provide some means of drainage for these areaways and to place a protecting grill or grating over the opening.

Another method sometimes used to turn surface water away from basement walls is to lay a concrete pavement, walk, or gutter, 2' or 3' in width around the house with a gradual slope away from the walls. Where the sidewalk joins the wall, the wall surface should be roughened, cleaned, and moistened, and the concrete rounded up to meet the face of the wall. This method will make a good bond and turn water away from the joint between the wall and sidewalk.

The gutter type of construction is used to conduct surface water along the wall to some low spot. The gutter should be at least 2' wide, with an outer lip or edge about 5" in width. The depression should be about 4" deep at the outer edge and sloped gradually up to meet the wall, and the joint should be treated in the manner recommended for the sidewalk.

Drains for Ground Water

In low, damp locations or in other places where there is a large amount of water in the subsoil, it is advisable to install drain tile around the footings to lower the water level and carry the water away before it can penetrate into the basement.

To lay the tile, dig a trench adjoining, and to a depth of a few inches below, the bottom of the basement floor, but not below the footing level. The tile should be at least 4" in diameter (although 3" tile has proved satisfactory in some cases) and should be laid so that the grade or fall will be smooth and as sharp as possible to avoid mud settling in the pipe. The tile should also be connected to an outlet similar to those recommended for downspouts. The cracks between the joints should be covered on top with copper screen wire or strips of roofing paper to prevent sediment from running into the pipe. The pipe should be carefully laid and protected against settling or leakage by surrounding it with fine screened gravel or broken stone, tamped firmly around it. Following this, coarser gravel up to 1" in size should be covered over the pipe to a depth of 1' or 2'. Before back-filling with earth to grade level, it is well to spread burlap or bagging or to place sod, grass side down, on top of the stone to prevent fine material falling or washing down into the stone.

If an outside drain is impracticable, some relief from flooding may be obtained by removing the basement floor near its junction with the walls and placing a drain along the inside edge of the footing. The drain should pass through or under the footing to an outlet that is open at all times. An alternate method frequently employed to handle water from leakage is to cut a trough in the floor leading the water to a sump with a drain or pump. The trough may be covered with a perforated cover. Where conditions are unusually bad, waterproofing may be necessary in addition to the drain.

Exterior Waterproofing

If waterproofing is necessary, it should be applied to the outside face of the wall before backfilling. Different methods can be used, depending largely upon local conditions. By applying the coating to the outside, water is prevented from entering the wall. The water pressure tends to force the coating into tighter contact. If the coating is placed on the inside, water pressure through the wall may force it away from the wall surface.

Cement-Mortar Coatings

Where ground-water conditions are not a major consideration and protection against dampness only is required, a coating of cement-mortar is usually applied over grout to the outside of masonry-unit walls. This coating consists of one, or preferably two, $\frac{3}{8}''$ coats of cement mortar composed of 1 part of Portland cement or 2 or 3 parts of sand by volume. The surface of the wall should first be cleaned and wetted until nearly saturated with water. While still damp, but without water showing on the surface, it should be scrubbed with a grout coat of Portland cement and water of the consistency of thick cream. Before this coating has set and while still wet, the first $\frac{3}{8}''$ trowel coat of cement mortar should be applied. Before this coat hardens, it should be scratched with a coarse broom or other tool to roughen the surface and provide a good bond for the second coat. On the following day, the first or scratch coat should be dampened, and the second $\frac{3}{8}''$ coat applied. The wall should be kept damp for three days or more.

Bituminous Coatings

Bituminous coatings, either hot- or cold-applied, will give protection where dampproofing only is necessary, provided the surfaces on which they are used are smooth. Rough walls should be given a grout coat of cement mortar and allowed to dry before the bituminous coating is applied. Bituminous coatings should be used only on the outside of either masonry-unit or monolithic walls because such coatings on the inside walls of basements are likely to blister or peel.

Cold-applied coatings may be of heavy-brushing or trowel consistency, with asphalt or coal-tar pitch as the base. Before applying brushed or troweled coatings, the wall should be primed, using an asphalt primer with asphalt coatings and a coal-tar or creosote primer with coal-tar coatings. Bituminous coatings may also be applied to cement-mortar coats.

Hot-applied coatings of asphalt or coal-tar pitch when properly applied are superior to cold-applied coatings, because they usually provide more bitumen per unit area than the cold-applied coatings. Walls should be smooth and dry and should be primed, using an asphalt primer for coal-tar pitch coatings. The hot-applied coatings are "mopped-on" with a roofer's mop, in one or more applications, to a thickness of at least $\frac{1}{8}''$.

When there is water pressure against the walls from a spring or other source, the most effective treatment for the walls is a so-called bituminous membrane. It is made with

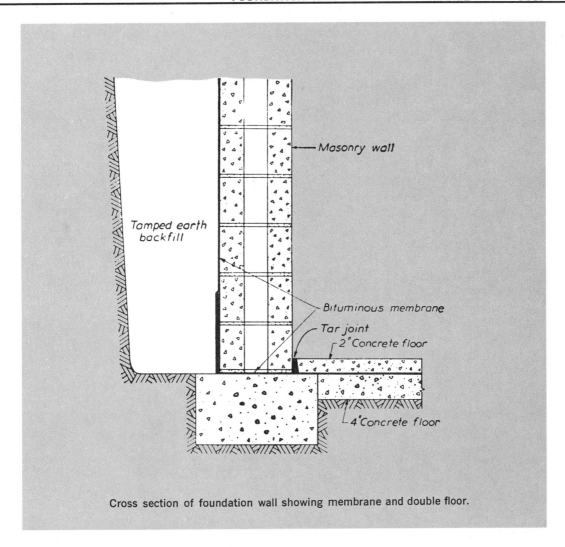

Cross section of foundation wall showing membrane and double floor.

three or more layers of asphalt or coal-tar saturated felt or fabric, cemented to the wall and to each other, and coated with asphalt or coal-tar pitch. Walls should be prepared as described for single hot-applied coatings.

Interior Waterproofing

Waterproof coatings are more effective when applied to the outer faces of the walls. However, if the water pressure from leakage is small, cement-mortar coatings may be applied successfully to the inside face. Active leaks through cracks may usually be sealed by plugging them with a cement mortar containing an accelerator to hasten hardening. The masonry around the crack should be cut away to a depth and width of 1″ or 2″. A stiff putty should then be prepared from high-early-strength Portland cement, sand, and calcium chloride up to 5% by weight of the cement. The mortar mix may be 1 part cement to 2 or 3 parts sand. The putty should be pressed into the opening and held by a small board or form until it has hardened

Four-Stroke Cycle

The power cycle on an engine which is concluded in four strokes. Here are the four phases or strokes necessary to produce the power:

1. On the downstroke, there is the intake, or the fuel is drawn into the cylinder.

2. Next, on the upstroke, there is compression—the fuel and air in the cylinder are pressed into a smaller volume.

3. Ignition and expansion occur in the third phase; after the mixture is ignited, it expands and drives the cylinder to produce the work of the motor.

4. In the final stroke, there is the exhaust—the ignited mixture which has burned passes out as smoke.

Fraction Equivalents

In going over estimates or bills you may find the figures in decimals, and it may be that you prefer to translate them into fractions for greater convenience. The way to do this is shown in the section on *DECIMAL EQUIVALENTS*.

Framing a Picture

It's easy to frame a picture. The only tools you need to do a professional-like job is a miter box, backsaw and a hammer. The moldings, readily available in lumber yards and in many hardware stores, come in many shapes and are priced at about 10c a foot and up. But you can make your own picture frame moldings from any straight-grained, knot-free wood. All you have to do is cut a rabbet into which the glass will be set. This can be done with a rabbet plane or hand saw or power tools.

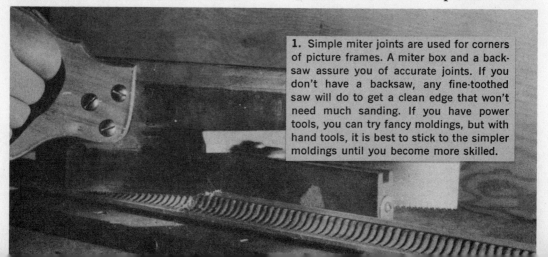

1. Simple miter joints are used for corners of picture frames. A miter box and a backsaw assure you of accurate joints. If you don't have a backsaw, any fine-toothed saw will do to get a clean edge that won't need much sanding. If you have power tools, you can try fancy moldings, but with hand tools, it is best to stick to the simpler moldings until you become more skilled.

2. Glue and a brad will be sufficient to hold most corners, except for large or heavy frames. If you have corner clamps, you can join the pieces together for a perfect fit, insert a brad and then glue the corner. It is best to fit all four corners at the same time; this will assure you of a perfectly square frame.

3. If you don't have corner clamps, you can make your own gluing jig. Use your workbench or a large board as a base. Fasten four large blocks along the outside perimeter of the picture frame, about ¼" from the outside edge. Small wooden wedges are used to lock the corners of the frame after the glue has been applied.

4. After the corners are set and the glue dry, remove the frame and sand off any excess glue. Fill any pits, cracks or nicks with wood filler. After the filler dries, sand with fine steel wool or sandpaper.

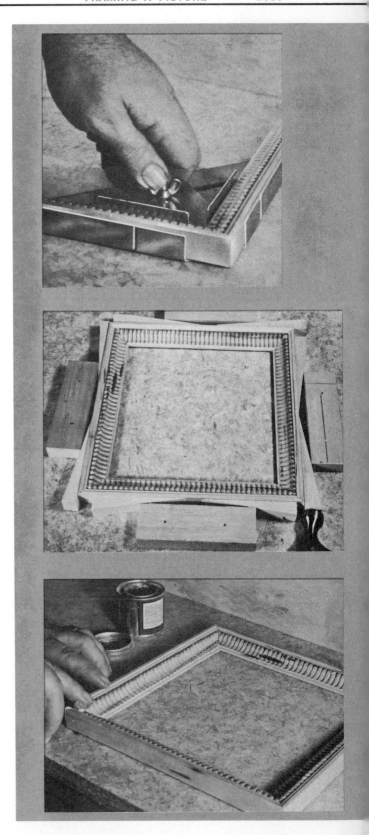

5. Brush the frame free of dust and you're ready to apply the finish. This is an exacting step and should be done carefully. You can paint the frame if you like, or you might prefer to stain it. For the different finished effects and techniques, see **Furniture—Finishing.**

6. When the finish is dry, take a piece of single-strength window glass—only large pictures need heavier glass—and lay it within the frame. Set the picture, and the matting if you use one with the picture, over the glass. Then cut a piece of cardboard to the same size as the glass and set it over the picture back. Now apply masking tape along the outside edges to hold the pieces within the frame and to make it dust-free.

7. To get the picture ready to hang, set two small screw eyes above the center on each side of the frame. A piece of fine wire or strong cord is then tied loosely between the two eyes.

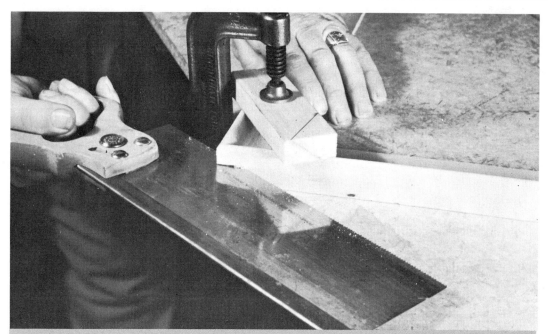

8. A spline joint at the corner makes for a stronger joint. This requires precision cutting but is necessary when you make large or heavy frames. Blind doweling can be used, but a spline is easier to make if you don't have a doweling jig. Clamp the two pieces together at the proper angle and saw a slot into the edge of the pieces.

9. Cut the corner spline out of a strip of hardwood; it should be about one-fourth the thickness of the frame. Slip the hardwood strip into the slot cut in the preceeding step, after applying a liberal coat of glue. When the glue is dry, saw off the excess of the strip with a fine-toothed saw. Then proceed as you would with a simple glue-and-brad corner.

Framing Braces

Special braces have been developed to speed framing by eliminating toe-nailing, notching and shimming. Among them are Teco Trip-L-Grips, made of 18-gage sheet steel, which are nailed in place with special anchors similar to 8d common nails.

These framing braces not only speed framing but increase the rigidity at the openings and corners. Special types are made for specific jobs and vary according to the load they will carry.

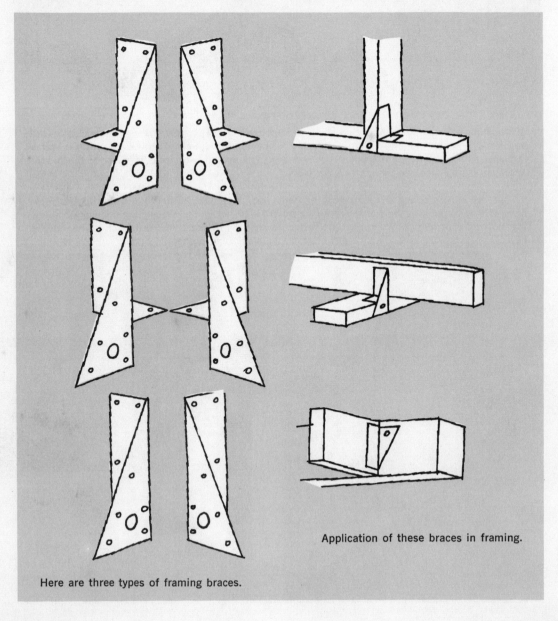

Here are three types of framing braces.

Application of these braces in framing.

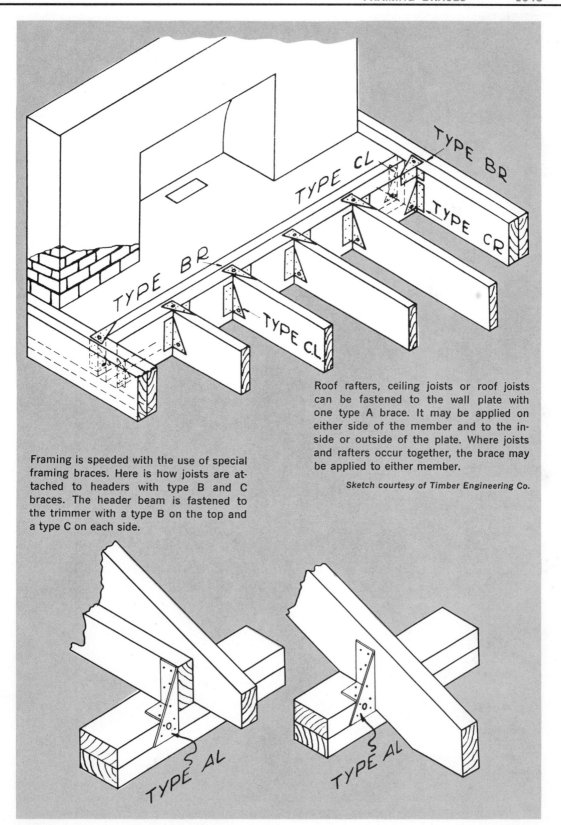

Framing is speeded with the use of special framing braces. Here is how joists are attached to headers with type B and C braces. The header beam is fastened to the trimmer with a type B on the top and a type C on each side.

Roof rafters, ceiling joists or roof joists can be fastened to the wall plate with one type A brace. It may be applied on either side of the member and to the inside or outside of the plate. Where joists and rafters occur together, the brace may be applied to either member.

Sketch courtesy of Timber Engineering Co.

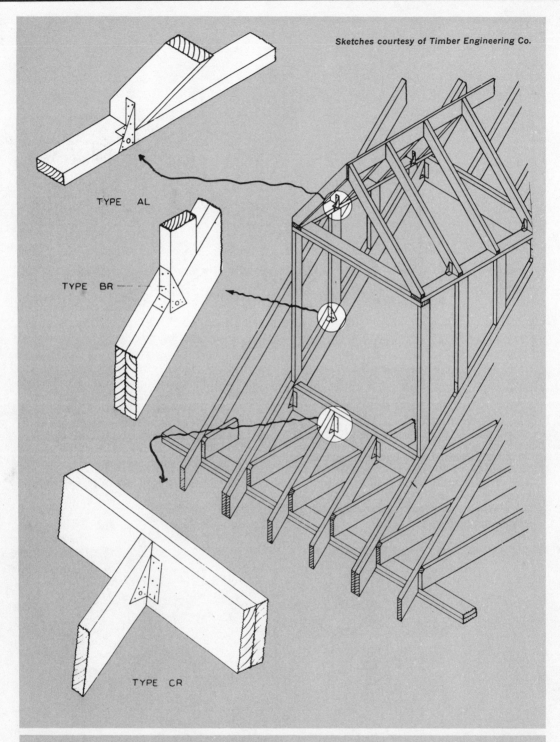

Sketches courtesy of Timber Engineering Co.

TYPE AL

TYPE BR

TYPE CR

Here is the framing for a dormer using framing braces instead of conventional cutting and toe-nailing. The rafters are fastened to the headers with one type C brace. The headers are fastened to the double rafters (or trimmer) with two type C braces at each end. It is best to fasten the alternate dormer studs to the double rafters with one type B brace. Finally, the dormer rafter is fastened to the plate with one type A brace.

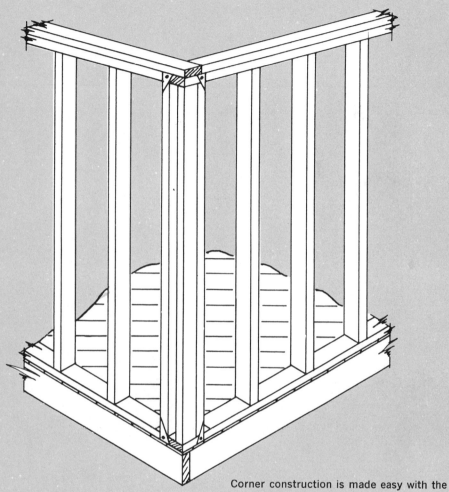

Corner construction is made easy with the special framing braces. Corner posts, built up or solid, can be fastened to the plate with one type BR and one type BL brace. Then the corner post is fastened to the sill with one type BR and one type BL brace.

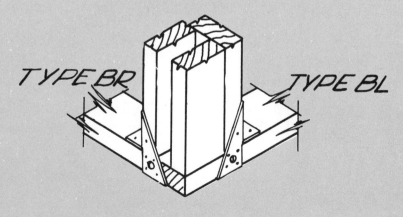

TYPE BR   TYPE BL

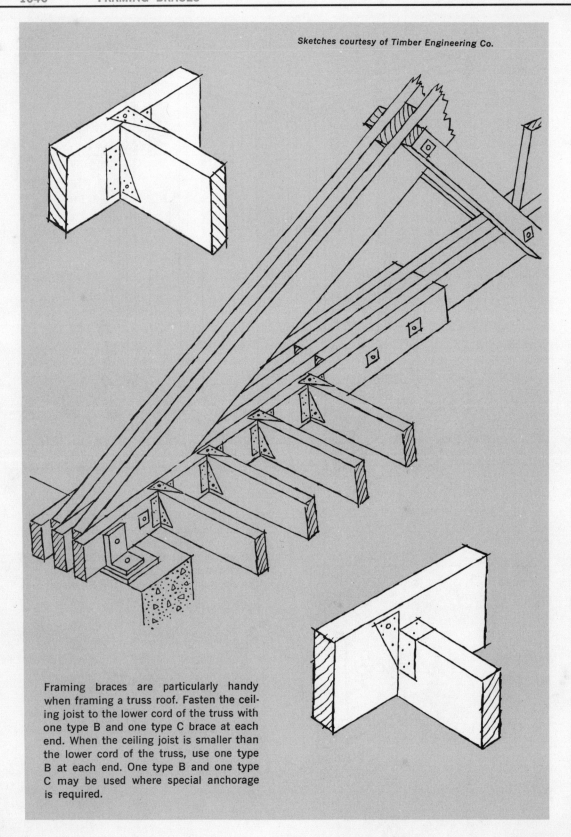

Sketches courtesy of Timber Engineering Co.

Framing braces are particularly handy when framing a truss roof. Fasten the ceiling joist to the lower cord of the truss with one type B and one type C brace at each end. When the ceiling joist is smaller than the lower cord of the truss, use one type B at each end. One type B and one type C may be used where special anchorage is required.

Among all the tools used by the professional carpenter there is, perhaps, none so simple and so indispensable as the framing square. It is, as well, a very useful tool for the handyman engaged in many projects.

The framing square is used to mark lines squarely across a board, to lay out the spacing for studs, etc., in construction work, to align two pieces at a right angle, and many

Framing Square

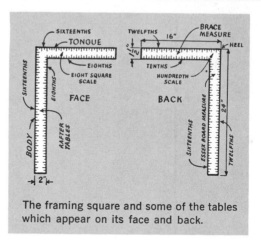

The framing square and some of the tables which appear on its face and back.

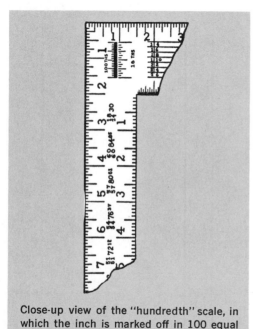

Close-up view of the "hundredth" scale, in which the inch is marked off in 100 equal parts and with the aid of a pair of dividers, fractions of an inch can be obtained easily and quickly.

other purposes. It is also used to determine easily and quickly the length of any common, hip, valley or jack rafter for any pitch of a roof. It can be used for determining the proper top and bottom cuts as well as side or cheek cuts for any rafter. There are many different scales on both the face and back of the framing square. Their use is involved and anyone interested in learning the many ways in which a framing square can be used can obtain informative booklets from the leading manufacturers of this tool.

Framing Systems

If your home interior is made primarily of lumber, it has been framed in one of three basic methods commonly used in the United States. The technique of framing to some extent varies regionally, and, to a

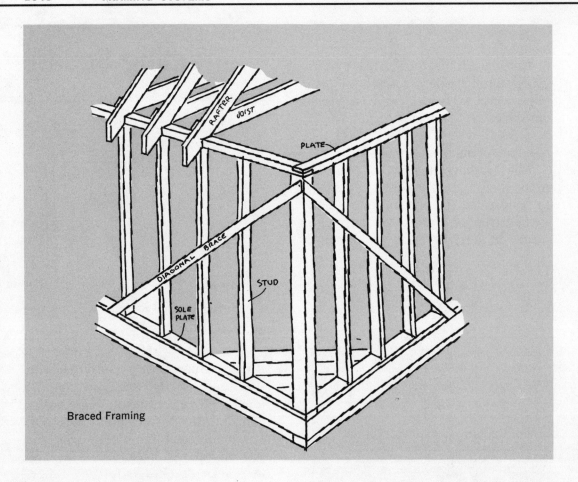

Braced Framing

lesser extent, upon the period in which the house was built.

The three basic types of framing are:

1. Eastern or braced—it is also known as old-fashioned braced, as the early buildings in New England, where this style was first used, were designed to last forever.

2. Balloon—this method of framing was developed to reduce the cost of framing and to save time in building.

3. Western or platform—this is a radical departure from the Eastern style and also differs from the balloon type of framing. It is lighter than the braced type of framing but is sturdier than the balloon type.

Braced Framing

In this system of framing, all the vertical structural elements of both bearing and partition walls, except for the corner posts, extend for one story only. The first floor wall members extend from the sill at the top of the foundation to the top plate. The second floor vertical members extend from the top plate of the first floor upward.

The corner posts in this type of framing extend from the foundation still right up to the roof plate. They are braced by diagonal members which usually extend the full height of each story. These diagonal members or braces cross several of the studs in each of the outer walls.

Balloon Framing

Unlike the braced framing, the vertical structural members of a balloon-framed house extend from the foundation sill to the roof plate as single pieces. The intermediate floor and ceiling joists are attached to these studs in bearing walls.

To support the floor of the second story, a ribband or ribbon is attached to one piece vertical studs. The joists run at right angles to the ribbons. Furthermore, diagonal bracing is sometimes omitted, although today the building codes often require that these braces be added in new homes being constructed with balloon frames.

Platform Framing

The primary difference in platform framing is the setting of the floor plates of one story directly upon the top plates of the story below it. The bearing walls and partition walls rest on the subfloor of each story.

Furthermore, there are two members not found in the other types. They are a header and a shoe or sole plate used for the outer walls. The headers are made of 2″ stock, the same depth as the joists, which rest on and are framed directly to the sill. The shoe or sole plate are horizontal members, usually 2x4's, and rest directly on the sub-floor.

French Polish

This polish may be bought in a brown color, as well as colorless which enhances the natural wood color. It is used on mahogany or any other wood where you want a lasting, mirrorlike gloss. Old-style French polish consists of a fine grade of shellac, which may be thinned with any shellac-mixing grade of denatured alcohol. Modern French polishes, which are much easier to use and are particularly convenient for touch-up and refinishing jobs, require a special thinner supplied by the manufacturers of the polish.

Select a room to work in where there is no dampness, and the temperature is evenly warm. Before applying the polish, it is necessary that the wood surface be clean, smooth, free of any cracks. The latter should be covered with a filler. A paste wood filler, too, should be used if the wood is porous. The surface should be sandpapered if there are any rough spots on the wood.

Use a small mop brush to flow the French polish onto the wood, and let it dry. As this is the first coat, you can determine now if the color produced by the polish is what you want; if not, you could change it to something more desirable. If the color is a little too light or too red, add a bit of spirit black to the French polish. If you want to make the color darker, add more coloring before you proceed with the next coat. Test these color first on a scrap of wood or the underside of the piece of furniture: never experiment on the exposed parts.

Before you go ahead with the second step, make a "surface rubber" by covering a wad of absorbent cotton with an old, soft cotton or linen cloth. This rubber is soaked in the French polish, and then a drop of linseed oil is placed on the pad if the old-style polish is being used. When the first coat on the wood has dried, go over the surface with this lubricated rubber in lines curved like the number 8. Do this from one end to the other vertically; then rub in the same manner horizontally. You will find that a film is produced.

Let the piece of furniture rest for several days; go over the surface with very fine sandpaper, and again proceed with the rubber in the same way as before. If you desire, this process may be repeated several times, but each time you will use less polish and more thinner until at the final time you actually use the rubber very lightly and quickly with clear alcohol.

It is important that this work be done meticulously. The rubber must be kept constantly in motion and must be kept in contact with the wood, as by raising it abruptly you might pick off some polish from the wood or roughen the surface. Should that occur, you would have to use sandpaper and go through it all again, right from the start.

Friction Catch

This hardware item is used on furniture and in cabinets to keep the doors closed—not locked. It usually consists of a plunger which fits into a spring or spring-steel jaw.

Also see *FURNITURE*.

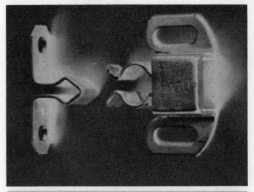

A friction catch normally used on kitchen cabinet and furniture doors.

Frost Line

The depth to which the soil freezes in a given locality is called the frost line. It is necessary to set the footing, or bottom course below the foundation, below the frost line.

If you are not certain as to the exact depth of the frost line in your community, you can get this information from your local building office, newspaper or the Weather Bureau station nearest your home.

Special paints are available in paint and hardware stores to make glass transluscent.

To frost glass, wash the surface with a clean cloth and warm water. Remove all dirt and, if necessary, use a scraper to remove any paint that might be on the glass.

Frosting Glass

Dry the glass thoroughly with a lint-free cloth. Then apply the liquid frosting with a paint brush as you would paint any surface.

Water pipes which are exposed to freezing temperatures should be covered, especially if located out of doors or in unheated spaces. Smaller water pipes are more likely to freeze than large waste or sewer pipes, since the latter carry water which has usually been warmed to some extent, and which flows off quickly, leaving the pipe empty.

Properties of Insulating Materials

Insulating materials for covering pipes should be fire-resistant and poor conductors of heat. Materials used for the purpose are corrugated or air-cell asbestos, 85% magnesite asbestos, and mineral wool and similar coverings. The insulation may be obtained in preformed shapes, as flexible rolls, or as a dry powder to be mixed with water to form a plastic cement coating which dries in place.

A description of how to apply some of these materials follows.

An air-cell pipe covering is made of layers of corrugated asbestos sheet wrapped in canvas. It is manufactured in sections 3′ long in the shape of hollow cylinders split lengthwise on one side so that each section may readily be placed around the pipe.

Frozen Pipes

Applying split pipe covering around pipes.

The covering is made in several thicknesses and for various sizes of pipe. Each section has a canvas lap to be pasted over the longitudinal joint and a canvas flap at one end to be pasted over the joint between sections. To further bind the covering and make it neat-looking, metal bands are placed about 18″ apart, over the joints between sections and around the middle of each section.

For insulating pipe fittings, such as valves, L's and T's, where the use of fabricated coverings is not practicable, asbestos cement or other refractory insulating cements may be used. They serve the same purpose as the pipe coverings because of their insulating and fire-resistant qualities.

The following tools and materials are needed: Steel tape measure, plasterer's trowel, hand saw, sharp pocket knife, pliers, metal tub or similar container for mixing cement, pan or dish for paste, and small, flat paint brush; asbestos air-cell covering for insulating pipes, asbestos cement, wire mesh, canvas, and paste.

The asbestos air-cell covering should be four-ply or 1″ thick. To estimate the quantity needed, the pipe between fittings to be covered should be measured and the measurements combined for each size of pipe to obtain the total linear feet for each size of covering. Metal band fasteners are furnished with the covering.

To estimate the quantity of asbestos cement needed to cover the pipes, the entire surface should be computed. A 100-lb. bag of cement will cover from 20 to 25 sq. ft. of surface to a thickness of 1″. Some brands of cement are also available in 10 lb. bags.

Sufficient 1″ wire mesh or "chicken wire" to cover the surface is necessary. The canvas should be of the same weight as that on the air-cell covering and large enough to enclose the cement covering around pipe fittings. The paste is the type sold by manufacturers of the covering material for pasting the canvas laps on air-cell coverings and for fastening canvas jackets over pipe fittings. The paste may be purchased ready-to-mix with cold water.

Asbestos Cement

Asbestos cement should be mixed thoroughly in a tub or large container, using only enough water to make the mixture workable. At least two coats should be applied to the pipe and fittings and this should be done at a time when the pipes are not too cold to insure best results. Each coat on the pipe should be ½″ thick. In all cases, the first coat should be applied roughly with the hands or with a plasterer's trowel, and the surface scratched to insure a good bond with the second coat.

Insulating Pipes

Before the pipes are covered, they should be clean and in good condition. The canvas lap on the pipe covering should be loosened and brushed along the edge with paste to refasten the lap.

The pipe should then be encased with a section of covering placed with the open side up and with the end which has no canvas-joint overlap placed right against the fitting and pressed closely together. Paste the lap securely over the longitudinal joint.

The second section should be applied in the same manner, and pushed tightly against the first. The joint between the two sections should be sealed by pasting the overlap attached to the first section over the joint. The pipe covering should be continued in this way until the next fitting is reached. When a short section is needed, the covering can be cut with a sharp knife and handsaw.

For the fittings, the first coat of asbestos cement should be applied with the hands to a thickness of about ½″. The next step is to finish

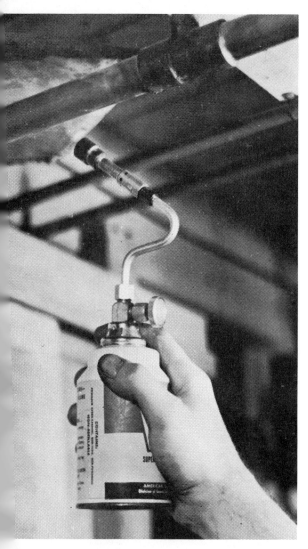

of lead-and-oil or other suitable paint in the desired color.

Metal bands to hold the pipe covering should be applied after all other work is completed, so they will be clean and present a neat finished appearance. The bands should be placed about 18″ apart, over the joints and midway between. They should be pulled up tightly and fastened with the pliers.

Underground Pipes

When pipes are laid underground they should be buried deep enough to be protected from damage by heavy vehicles passing over them and to eliminate the danger of freezing. The depth depends on climate and local soil conditions.

the covering by the application of a ½″ second coat or one of the same thickness as the pipe covering. This coat should be troweled smooth and beveled down to meet the surface of the pipe covering.

Asbestos cement on the fittings will be protected and will present a neat appearance if covered with a canvas jacket. The canvas should be of the same weight as that used on the pipe covering, and should be pasted down smoothly. To look well and preserve the canvas, it should be sized and painted with two coats

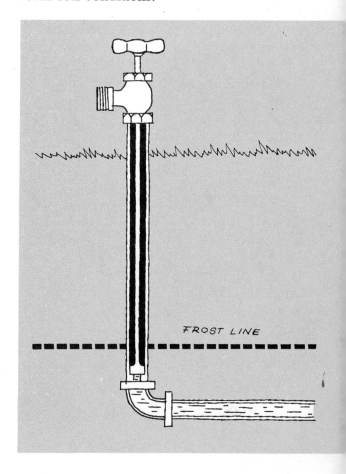

FROST LINE

Frost protection in the central and northern latitudes of the United States usually requires that pipe be placed from 2½' to 3' in the ground. In the extreme Northern States, it is well to go as deep as 4' to 6', and in the Southern States a depth of from 1½' to 2' is usually enough covering to protect the pipe from damage.

Also see *FROST LINE*.

Thawing Pipes and Drains

If water-supply pipes become frozen, they should be promptly thawed out to avoid possible bursting. In lead and soft copper pipes, a bulge in the pipe will disclose the location of the frozen area, whereas, in other metals, no such bulge will appear.

Some form of heat will be required to melt the ice in the pipes. The heat may be applied to the exterior of a frozen pipe by electrical resistance, direct flame, or hot applications of water or steam. In thawing out water pipes, it is best to work toward the supply end, keeping a faucet open to indicate when the flow starts. When thawing out a waste or sewer pipe, it is best to start at the lower end and work upward, to allow the water to flow off as the ice is melted.

In heating frozen water-supply pipes by electrical resistance, a source of low voltage, such as a welding generator, should be connected directly to the water pipe with the two electrical conductors clamped to the pipe to span the frozen section. As soon as a section has been thawed out, the conductors should be moved along the pipe to thaw another section. A welding shop, or a plumber who has electrical thawing equipment, should be called to perform this work.

Direct flame may be applied to frozen pipes with a blow torch, provided there is no danger of burning the adjoining woodwork. The flame should be played gradually along the pipe to spread the heat evenly. Try a heat lamp for this job—there's no flame but plenty of heat.

Hot applications on a frozen pipe do not produce as quick results as direct flame, but like a heat lamp, are much safer because they lessen the fire hazard and the possibility of bursting the pipe.

Other methods of hot application may be used if the water pipes are accessible. They can either be wrapped with cloths and saturated with boiling water or the boiling water can be poured directly over the pipe. In both cases, a receptacle should be placed below the pipe to catch the water.

Steam, used by plumbers to thaw out pipes, is provided by a steamer resembling a 5-gallon oil can, having a hose and nozzle attached. The steamer is heated by a furnace.

Frozen traps, waste pipes, drains, and sewer pipes may be opened by pouring boiling water into them through the drain opening or trap. If this is not successful, a can of lye or drainpipe cleaner dissolved in two gallons of cold water in a porcelain container should be poured carefully into the drain opening or trap. Do not use hot water with lye or cleaner and avoid splashing the solution on face, hands or clothing.

A complete row of bricks laid across a wall with only the ends exposed.

Also see *BRICKS*.

Full Header

Fuller Faucet

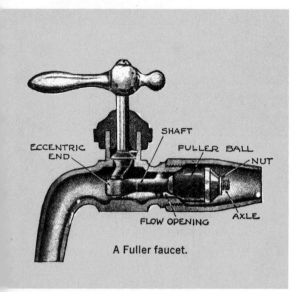

A Fuller faucet.

A faucet, not frequently used today, in which the flow of water is stopped by means of a small rubber ball which is forced into the seat or opening connected to the inlet pipe.

Also see *FAUCET*.

Fumed Finish

While it has been popular to think of "fumed oak," actually other woods, such as mahogany and walnut, may also be finished in this manner. The process of fuming is such, however, that it may not be feasible to produce the finish on very large pieces.

It is necessary to provide a container (perhaps a closet) which is absolutely air-tight. Place the wood pieces into this container, in which are set a few dishes of liquid ammonia. As the wood absorbs the ammonia vapors it becomes a deep brown color. If you want the color to be deeper and richer, the wood should remain in this airtight container a longer time.

After the wood has become "fumed" to the desired color, it should be taken out, and then you may finish it as you wish.

A simulated fuming is sometimes produced by wiping the wood with ammonia. However, this is not as satisfactory as the result obtained through the absorption of the fumes.

Fumigants, Disinfectants, Insecticides— Hazards

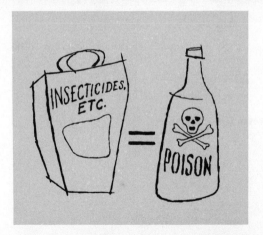

A fumigant is a gaseous product used for the destruction of insect or germ life; a disinfectant is a powder, liquid, or gas that destroys disease germs or renders them harmless; an insecticide is a gas, powder, or liquid used for the destruction of insects, rodents, etc. A disinfectant is not necessarily an insecticide, as some powerful disinfectants are relatively harmless for insects, and good insecticides may be of little value as disinfectants. Formaldehyde is a powerful disinfectant, but it is a very weak insecticide; and, conversely, hydrocyanic acid is deadly for insects and all forms of animal life, but it has little power as a disinfectant.

Hydrocyanic Acid Gas

Fumigation with hydrocyanic acid gas is one of the most effective methods of destroying household insects. This gas is, however, extremely poisonous to human beings and should not be used without knowledge of the dangers involved and of the precautions to be taken. Fatal accidents have occurred from such a careless act as going in to a room or house while the place was being fumigated with hydrocyanic acid gas.

The pot method, which consists of placing sodium cyanide in a mixture of sulphuric acid and water in an earthenware crock or in a barrel, is the most common method of fumigation by hydrocyanic gas. Other methods involve the use of various forms of calcium cyanide or liquid hydrocyanic acid, either pure or combined with some absorbent material. Any method of fumigation with hydrocyanic gas should be performed under expert direction and with full observance of the instructions contained in Government publications.

Formaldehyde

A solution of formaldehyde is an excellent and reliable disinfectant. It is an excellent deodorant as well as a disinfectant and may be usefully employed for disinfecting small areas about the house and for disinfecting discharges from the sickroom. While relatively not very poisonous, it does have a very penetrating odor and the gas is irritating to the eyes and respiratory organs.

Carbolic Acid

The term "carbolic acid" is rather loosely employed to designate a variety of substances which, though related chemically, are very different in their disinfecting properties. In a pure state true carbolic acid or phenol is solid at ordinary temperatures and when freed of water crystallizes in long white needles. Because of their property of absorbing water from the air, the crystals are likely to form a solid cake in bottles and other containers. For this reason, drug stores usually dispense carbolic acid in a liquid form prepared by adding one part of water to nine parts of crystals. Carbolic acid is not as powerful as other cheaper disinfectants. It is very poisonous and is also objectionable because its strong odor is absorbed by foods. It should be kept in clearly labeled or special shaped containers and stored in cabinets provided for such chemicals.

Cresol

Cresol is found on the market in varying degrees of purity. It is also known under a variety of names such as tricresol, cresylic acid, liquid carbolic acid, etc. It has a strong odor resembling that of pure carbolic acid and, like carbolic acid, is very poisonous and corrosive. Cresol may be used in the same way as pure carbolic acid, though it is considerably more powerful as a disinfectant and is therefore employed in a weaker solution. Because of its odor, it should not be used in or near compartments where foods are kept.

Chlorinated Lime

Bleaching powder (chlorinated lime) is a white powder that gives off the disagreeable odor of chlorine. It should be kept in hermetically sealed containers because exposure to the air causes it to deteriorate rapidly. The efficiency of chlorinated lime is largely dependent upon the quantity of available chlorine it contains. Although chlorinated lime is a very powerful disinfectant, its potency is immediately and greatly reduced when it is brought into contact with organic matter. For general household use 6 ounces of chlorinated lime are mixed with 1 gallon of water.

Besides chlorinated lime, other similar chlorine compounds such as sodium hypochlorite are in more or less common use as disinfectants. The uses to which chlorine disinfectants may be put are restricted because of their corrosive action and their odor. They are powerful bleaching agents and corrode metal. The odor of chlorine disinfectants is likely to be absorbed by foods, and for this reason such disinfectants should not be used in or near food compartments.

Corrosive Sublimate

Corrosive sublimate (mercuric chloride) is very poisonous, and its use about the household is not recommended. The United States Department of Agriculture states that corrosive sublimate is not nearly so effective or satisfactory for household use as other disinfectants, such as formaldehyde.

Other Chemicals

In addition to fumigants and disinfectants, which may also be used for killing insects and rodents, cer-

tain other dangerous chemicals may be used for this or other specific household purposes. White arsenic (arsenious oxide) is used as a poison for flies and rodents. It is an essential constitutent of Paris green and London purple which are extensively used as insecticides in vegetable gardens. These insecticides also contain copper, which is poisonous. They should be handled with considerable care. Barium carbonate, also used as a constituent or rodent poison, presents the same sort of hazard as arsenious oxide but in a less degree.

Phosphorous, sometimes used as a rodent poison, should not be used because of its double hazard of fire and poison. Alkaloids, such as strychnine, should not be used for rodent poison because of the extreme dangers involved in careless or mistaken use. Carbon bisulfide, frequently used as a constituent of rubber cement and for killing ants, is not extremely poisonous, but its use involves a fire hazard because its vapor can be ignited by contact with a steam pipe or other object at a temperature far below red heat.

Nicotine Sulphate

Nicotine sulphate is sometimes used as an insecticide, and instances are known where persons have been severely injured by inhalation or by absorption by the skin of the fog or spray. Therefore, when using nicotine sulphate or other nicotine insecticides, one should not stand on the windward side of the spray. Other precautions recommended by the National Institute of Health and by the United States Department of Agriculture should be observed.

DDT

See separate section on *DDT HAZARDS*.

Furnace

See *HEATING SYSTEMS*.

Furniture Basic Primer

The handyman can make his own good furniture by following building plans. Power tools help to make the job easier and quicker. However, even with hand tools, you will be able to build many fine additions for your home.

Designing furniture is an art. Even if you don't have this skill, you can, nonetheless, make your own plans for a piece of furniture you wish to duplicate by applying the methods and techniques in this section.

In this section you will find a primer of design and techniques. It is planned to help you understand how different parts are put together, to understand the construction principles and to make use of these when copying any piece of furniture.

Making furniture can provide many hours of enjoyment for the members of your family. You can recruit them and put them to work in the assembly and finishing of the pieces. It is important to realize, before starting any project, that good furniture cannot be made without accurate measurement, exact cutting and precision joining. Rushing a job may ruin many hours of hard work. It is best to plan the job completely and collect the necessary tools and materials before starting on a project.

Materials and Methods

Which materials and what methods you use depend upon the type of furniture you are planning to build. A piece made for a year or two's use about the home or one which will be painted, need not be made of fine wood. On the other hand, if you plan to 'live' with the piece of furniture for many years, you should use select hardwoods finished in a craftsmanlike manner.

It takes the same amount of time and effort to make good furniture out of fine wood as it takes to make the furniture out of poor wood. Even though hardwoods are more expensive than softwoods, the extra cost is a negligible factor in the long run.

While fir plywood or hardboard can be used in many projects, explore the possibilities of using hardwood-veneered plywood. Similarly, pine can be used for a furniture project, but hardwood—birch, oak, mahogany, etc.—will produce better-looking and longer-wearing furniture.

Just as you have a choice of woods, you have a choice of techniques. When making joints, it's fast and easy to use nails. But if you want the furniture to be more than slapped-together fruit boxes; it is better to make more professional-looking joints where the fastening method is concealed.

Woods You Can Use

When making your own furniture, you have a wide selection of materials to use. In addition to fir plywood and the hardwood-ve-

	Type of Wood	Color	Grain	Strength*
LEAST EXPENSIVE	Alder	Light pinkish brown to white	Mostly obscure	2
	Ash	Light grayish brown	Marked	1
	Beech	Very light red to brown	Hardly noticeable	1
	Chestnut	Grayish brown; the sapwood is white	Pronounced	2
	Elm	Light grayish brown, sometimes tinted with red	Marked	1
	Gum—Red	Reddish brown to pinkish white	Trace	2
	Maple—Western	Light tan to reddish brown	Faint	2
	Philippine Mahogany	Light to dark reddish brown	Ribbon pattern	2
	Poplar—Yellow	Light yellow to off white	Obscure	3
MEDIUM COST	Birch	Very light to dark reddish brown	Striped to curly	1
	Cherry	Light to dark reddish brown	Obscure	2
	Hickory	Light brown	Trace	1
	Mahogany—African	Very pale to dark reddish brown	Ribbon	2
	Maple—Eastern	White to light reddish brown	Figured	1
	Oak—Red	White to gray-reddish brown	Pronounced	1
	Walnut	Light to dark brown with gray cast	Pronounced	1
HIGH COST	Ebony	Black	None	1
	Primavera	Light yellow to white	Ribbon or figured	2
	Rosewood	Light red to moderate vermilion	High contrast	1
	Teak	Golden brown	Pronounced	1

* Strength ratings: 1—high strength, 2—medium strength, 3—low strength.

neered plywoods, you have panel materials, such as smooth-surfaced hardboard, textured hardboard, flat reinforced fiber glass, perforated hardboard and other panel materials. You can use any of the plastic laminates—Formica, Micarta, Consoweld, to name but a few, as well as ceramic tiles, rubber tile, cork, and Venetian glass tiles.

There are many woods which will greatly enhance the beauty of the furniture you make. Here is a partial list, classified somewhat arbitrarily by price, together with some notations about color and grain. High-grade lumber suitable for furniture is expensive and prices vary greatly. The price per board foot of carefully selected, kiln-dried, dressed lumber for cabinetwork is much lighter than wood of the same kind bought unselected and not surfaced on four sides.

Good Design

Anyone who plans and builds his own furniture will find a knowledge of design helpful. Even if you modify a plan you already have, an understanding of design principles will help produce a better job.

Any piece of furniture you design or build should meet three requirements. It should be useful, durable and attractive.

The size of a piece of furniture is generally determined by its use. For example a dining table should be 30″ high; the back of a chair should slope to form a 105° angle with the seat. Anatomical dimensions as well as building standards play a major role in design. See *ANATOMY FOR BUILDING.*

To be durable, it is necessary to make the piece of furniture out of sturdy wood with secure joints. Many techniques are included in this section. Also see *ADHESIVES, JOINTS, NAILS, SCREWS, DOWELS* and *LUMBER.*

The division of space in a pleasing manner makes a piece of furniture attractive. Even the finest woods, the best finish and professional workmanship combined cannot make a piece attractive if it does not have the proper proportions.

Here, in sketch form, are a few of the basic rules for designing and planning the division of space. See accompanying sketches, "Basic Proportions."

Basic Proportions

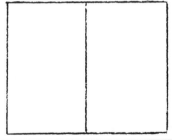

1. If a vertical line divides the space in two, one method you can follow is to make two sections of equal size.

2. On the other hand, you can divide the space in two by a vertical line so that one section is one and one-half times greater than the other.

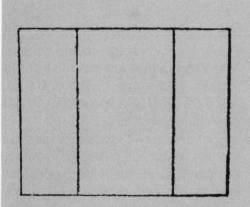

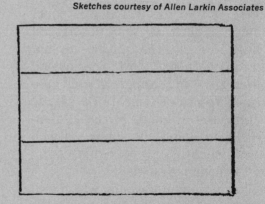

Sketches courtesy of Allen Larkin Associates

3. If vertical lines divide the space into three sections, the center one should be larger than either of the other two, which should be equal to each other.

4. If horizontal lines divide the space into three sections, the center one should be the largest and the other two should not be equal. The lower one should be larger than the upper one.

How To Join Boards

Often when making furniture, it is not possible to get boards wide enough to make large flat surfaces or sides. While it is possible to use plywood, you may prefer to use solid lumber. There are several ways in which to join boards to obtain one large one.

1. The straight butt joint is one of the simplest and most frequently used. All boards are jointed, that is, the edges planed so that they are square with the face or flat side of the board. Adhesive is applied along the edges and the boards are locked together with clamps until the adhesive has set.

2. Rabbet joints are more difficult to make and, therefore, less frequently used. To make this joint, it

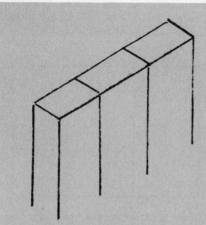

1. Butt joint method of joining boards.

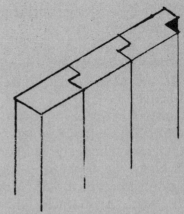

2. Rabbet joint is difficult to make unless you have power tools and are reasonably proficient in operating them.

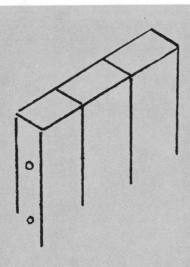

3. Dowel joint is simple and popular; it involves the use of blind doweling plus adhesives.

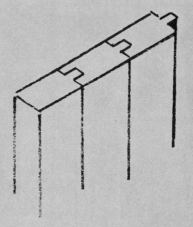

4. Tongue-and-groove joints are exceedingly practical if you have a shaper or a shaper attachment for your power saw or drill press.

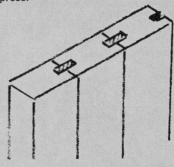

5. Feather or spline joint is one of the most practical and can be made even with hand tools. A dado plane can be used to cut the grooves for the spline.

is necessary to joint all boards and then cut a rabbet on each edge, except for the outside edges of the first and last board. The individual boards are secured with adhesive and clamps.

3. Dowel joining of individual pieces to make one large board is used often, especially with large surfaces. A blind dowel technique is employed to join the boards edge to edge. See *BLIND DOWELING* and *ADHESIVES.*

4. Tongue-and-groove joints are practical only if you have a shaper or shaper attachment to cut the tongue and groove along the edges of each board. The pieces are joined with adhesives and clamps.

5. The feather joint or spline technique is one of the most practical ways to join individual, small boards. This joint requires the use of power tools. Each cut has to be exact and hardwood must be used for the

'feathers' or 'splines.' Again, it is necessary to use adhesive and clamps.

6. A modified tongue-and-groove technique can be used. The ends of the boards are cut with a tongue and a narrow end piece or cleat is cut with a groove. This transverse rail, which runs at right angles to the boards, tends to eliminate any tendency toward warping. It is fastened with adhesives to the boards and adhesive is also used between the edges of the boards.

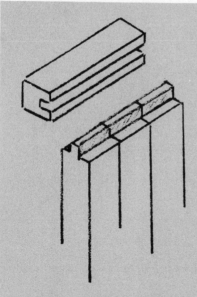

6. Modified tongue-and-groove method helps eliminate warping. Adhesive is used to fasten the transverse cleat along each edge and between the individual boards.

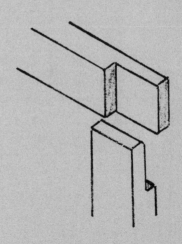

1. Although the end lap joint is easy to make, it is rarely found in good furniture. The joint is often reinforced with screws, or even bolts, plus adhesive.

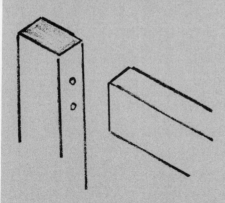

2. Dowel joints are fairly common and frequently used to attach a leg to a frame. While the dowels can be driven in from the outside edge, it is best to use the blind doweling technique for furniture making.

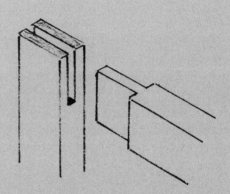

3. A through mortise and tenon is often used by the handyman but less frequently found in professionally built furniture. This joint is easy to make with a power saw with a dado head.

How To Join a Corner

Making a corner is an elementary part of furniture building. No matter what type of furniture you are making, you will encounter numerous corner joints. Of course, a simple butt joint where one piece fits flush against the other can be used. However, this is not a good furniture joint. Here is a choice of several different types of corner joints.

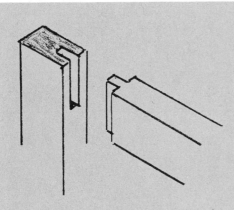

4. The open mortise and tenon looks more professional and is stronger than the through mortise and tenon. The mortise can be cut with a mortising chisel on a drill press.

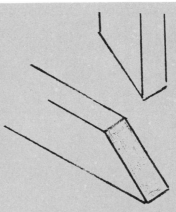

5. The conventional mitered joint with its 45° angle is not advised for any corner which will be subject to unusual strain or excessive weights. This joint is best to use on trim around cabinet doors and elsewhere, rather than at the primary corners of the furniture piece.

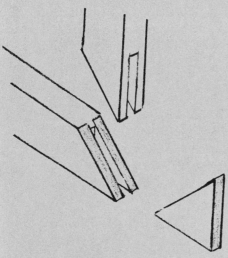

6. A miter joint with a spline, which is much stronger, can be made by the amateur. The joint is cut in the regular manner, then a groove is cut in each end and a spline inserted. Secure with adhesive.

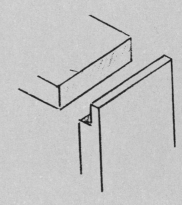

7. A rabbet is frequently used for joining the top of a piece of furniture to the sides. Whether cut in the side piece or the top piece, the rabbet leaves only a narrow strip of end grain visible.

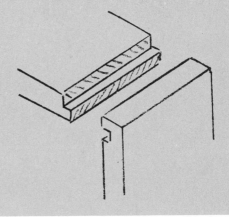

8. A box corner is sometimes used when making furniture, but the handyman is advised against this type of a joint since there is always a strong possibility of cracks along the edges.

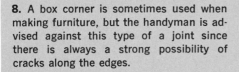

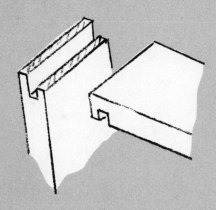

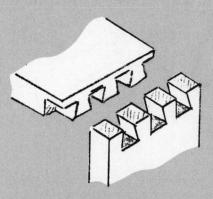

9. A milled corner joint is used extensively in the making of drawers. It is much stronger than the box corner joint and less subject to cracking; it has closed edges.

10. A half-blind dovetail joint is not recommended for the handyman without power tools. This joint is often used when making drawers and is very strong when held with adhesive.

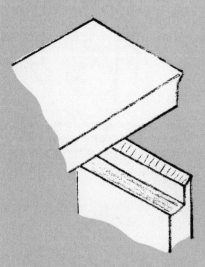

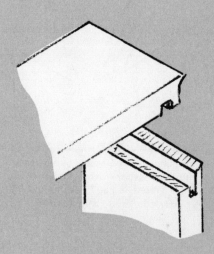

11. A mitered rabbet joint is easy to make with a power saw and looks professional. The pieces may be secured with dowels, screws or nails in addition to adhesive.

12. A lock miter joint is one of the better types for the experienced handyman to use when making furniture. The pieces must be cut accurately on a power saw. They are held securely with adhesive.

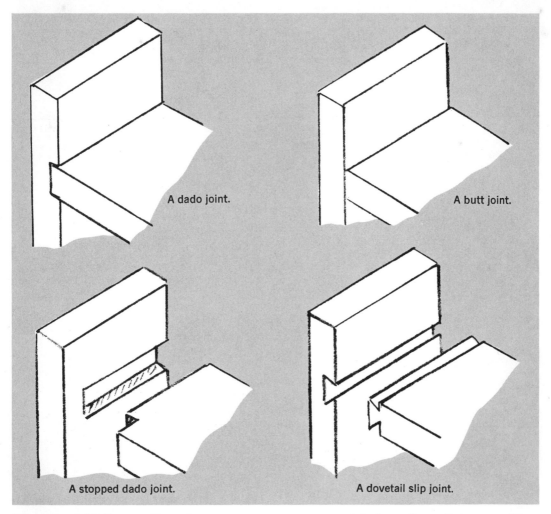

A dado joint.

A butt joint.

A stopped dado joint.

A dovetail slip joint.

How To Add Center Boards

When making a bookcase or a frame for a sofa, shelves or center support boards must be added. Here are four ways to do this job:

1. For a butt joint cut the shelf or center board to fit between the two sides. The board is then secured with nails or screws and adhesive. This type of a joint is not very strong and will not support any extensive weight.

2. A dado joint is much stronger and looks more workmanlike. The dado can be cut with a dado head on a power saw, a dado plane, a back-

saw, chisel and mallet or with a router. The center board or shelf is held with adhesive and, if necessary, countersunk screws or counterset nails.

3. A stopped dado joint is more difficult to make by hand. It looks better than the ordinary dado for the front edge of the side upright is uncut. It combines the finished appearance of a butt joint with the strength of a dado joint.

4. A dovetail slip joint is exceedingly strong and is best cut with a power saw. If this method is used, there is little chance of the sides pulling apart.

How To Add Panels

Panels are added to frames to make cabinet backs or doors. The material you use depends upon the location of the panel.

If the panel is used for the cabinet back and will not be visible, you can use hardboard or ¼" plywood. However, if the panel in the back will be visible, it might be better to use boards joined together or a decorative hardboard or a hardwood-veneered plywood.

If the panel is used for a door, you can make it out of joined boards, hardwood-veneered plywood, decorative hardboard, corrugated fiber glass or plate glass.

Here are but a few of the ways in which panels can be secured to a frame:

1. The panel can be mounted flush with the back, extending to the outer edges of the sides top and bottom. The panel can be fastened with adhesive, nails or screws.

2. The rear pieces can be cut with a rabbet to receive the panel. It is best to cut all the pieces—top, sides and bottom—before they are assembled, although with a router, this job can be done after the pieces are securely joined.

3. Easier for the handyman is the use of cleats attached to the inside of the sides, top and bottom. The cleats can be made out of finished molding, ½"x½" or larger, or quarter-round molding. The panel fits flush within the opening made by the top, sides and back.

4. The panel can be set in a simple dado or groove cut into the top, sides and bottom edges of the frame. The width of the dado should

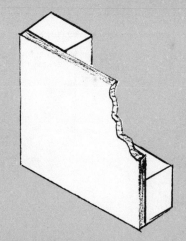

Flush mounting of the panel so that edges of the panel are flush with outside edges of both sides, top edge of top piece and lower edge of bottom piece.

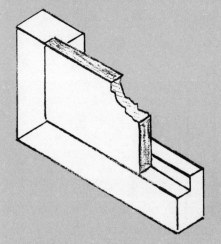

A rabbet cut into the top, sides and bottom forms a recess into which a panel can be set. Cut the rabbet before the basic parts of the frame are jointed.

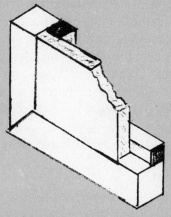

Cleats attached inside the cabinets provide an easy way to mount a panel. The cleats should be finished molding, either square stock or quarter round.

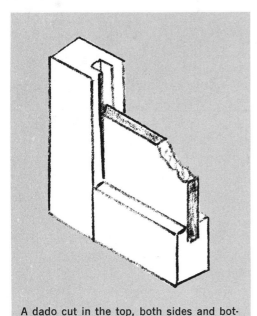

A dado cut in the top, both sides and bottom should be wide enough to accommodate the thickness of the panel material. The frame is an independent unit and holds rather than fastens panel in place.

be the same as the thickness of the panel used.

Adding Legs or a Base

A finished piece of furniture does not rest directly upon the floor. Either legs of some sort are added or a base is anchored to the underside of the unit.

Although wrought iron legs are very popular, many people still prefer to use wooden legs even with modern furniture. Some of the wooden legs come equipped with a steel plate which is fastened to the underside of the furniture unit with screws; the wooden leg is fastened to the steel plate with a hanger bolt.

Here are several ways to add legs to units when you cut the furniture leg yourself.

1. Simple butt joint can be used at the corner to join the two rails and the leg. Blind dowels plus adhesive will make a good job. This is the joint most handymen prefer to make because of its simplicity and ease in assembly.

2. A well-fitted open mortise and tenon makes a stronger joint. Tenons are cut on the ends of both rails and the adjoining faces of the leg are mortised to receive the rails. This type joint should be secured with adhesive, plus nails or screws when necessary.

3. The dovetail corner joint is exceptionally strong. It is one of the best methods for the handyman to use. This joint, however, should be cut with power tools. While it is possible to cut the joint by hand, it must be so precise only an experienced woodworker can do the job.

4. A gusset or glue block set in the corner not only joins the two rails but in some cases provides a larger surface to which to attach a leg. This method can be used to make a base; the base is then secured to the underside of the furniture unit by flathead screws driven upward through the gusset.

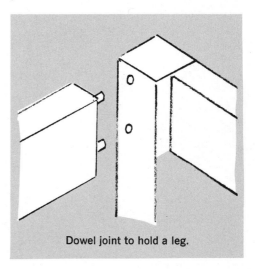

Dowel joint to hold a leg.

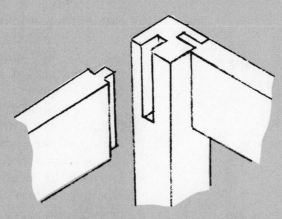

Open mortise and tenon is a stronger joint than the simple butt type.

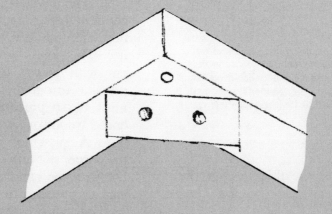

A gusset or glue block is used to fasten the two rails together. It sometimes provides a larger surface area for attaching a leg, and is often used on furniture bases to provide a ready means for fastening the base to the underside of the furniture.

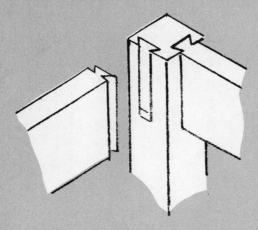

The dovetail corner joint is exceptionally strong and recommended for the handy-man skilled with power tools.

How To Treat an Edge

When working with plywood, it is often necessary to make some provision for concealing the edge. The edge view of plywood shows the many layers it takes to make up the sheet.

If the plywood is to be painted, there is no problem. All that is necessary is to fill the edge with wood filler, sand when dry and then paint.

On the other hand, if you wish to stain the edge of plywood, you cannot apply the stain directly. The end grain would 'drink' up the stain and you'd wind up with a very dark edge. You can apply a thin coat of shellac over which the stain can be applied. For techniques see section on *FURNITURE FINISHING*.

In the accompanying sketch are five ways to cover the edge of plywood. This is particularly necessary when you have used hardwood—veneered plywood.

Press-On Plywood Tape

Concealing the edges of plywood by adding a strip of thin veneer of matching wood used to be a job reserved for the experienced cabinetmaker. The handyman can now buy at his lumber yard or hardware store, a special thin self-adhering veneer of matching wood. It comes ¾" wide and in pieces up to 8' long. Here, in picture form, is how to apply this tape:

Note: for new type plywood edging see *PLYWOOD*.

Edge Treatment for Plywood

1. A thin veneer strip—1/16" or less—is glued to the edge of the plywood panel.

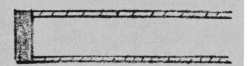

2. A solid strip of wood, ¼" to ½" thick and wide enough to cover the plywood, is fastened along the edge with counterset brads and adhesive.

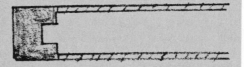

3. Tongue-and-groove technique is used to provide a better bonding surface for this edge. The solid strip can be the same wood as the surface of the plywood or of a contrasting color.

4. Tongue-and-groove technique is used but differs from the one just noted. Here the tongue is cut on the edge board and the groove cut in the plywood. The outside edge of the board can be bevelled or chamfer cut.

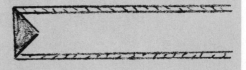

5. A mitered edge is used with extra fine work. A piece of the surface material or contrasting color wood is glued into a V-notch. This type of edge treatment requires precision cutting with power tools.

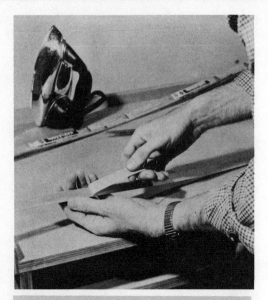

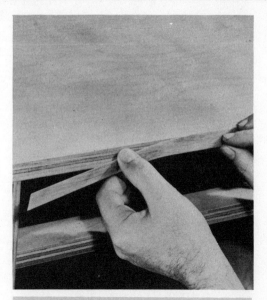

1. When you are ready to apply the tape edging, remove the tape (it comes in 7 different species of wood) from the cellophane wrapping. Holding it in one hand, strip off the protective backing from the adhesive side. It is best to use your thumb to prevent the wood from splitting—it's only about 1/32" thick.

2. Press the wood edging onto the plywood. Do this carefully to make certain that the same amount of excess extends above the surface of the plywood as below. Only light pressure is needed—just enough to keep the tape from falling off the edge. It can be cut with a pair of scissors or a dovetail saw or backsaw.

3. Heat is necessary to activate the adhesive for a positive bond of the tape to the plywood edge. There's no gluing or clamping. Just pull out the electric iron, heat it and pass it over the tape. Light, heat, about 250°, is needed for fir and mahogany, while moderate heat, about 300°, is needed for birch, oak and walnut.

4. A bonding iron is available for quick bonding of the tape to the plywood edge. There is little guesswork when you use this specially designed heating iron. Many stores selling the tape also rent the bonding iron. The iron is particularly useful around curves where it is difficult to make full contact with an ordinary electric iron.

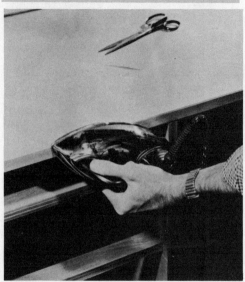

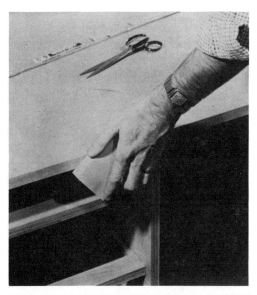

5. After the tape is bonded to the plywood edge, use 000 sandpaper with a block and sand the edges smooth with the surfaces of the plywood. Bevel the edges slightly but do not press too heavily. It is best to apply a finish coat shortly after the tape is applied. Water stain should not be used nor should the tape remain unfinished if you wish to maintain a perfect bond.

How To Conceal Screw Heads

Adhesive should be combined with either nails or screws when they are used in making any furniture joints.

Finishing nails should be used so that the heads may be set below the surface of the wood and the small holes filled with wood putty.

The heads of screws should also be concealed. It is best, therefore, to use flathead screws, unless otherwise called for in specific plans.

The head of the flathead screw can be concealed if a countersink bit is used when making the pilot holes or screws. Here are several ways in which flathead screws can be used:

1. The screw head can be driven so that the top is flush with the surface of the wood. This is all right for a back panel, but most people do not like to see the exposed head of a flathead screw.

2. The head can be driven deeper into the wood and the hole above it filled with wood filler to conceal the head.

3. However, most wood fillers are not difficult to finish so that they do not stand out from the rest of the surface. Therefore, a hole large enough to receive the head of the screw is bored deep enough to provide for a plug. The wood plug can be made out of a dowel or cut out of the same wood stock as the surface with a plug cutter. The plug is secured with adhesive. You can, if you use the same wood to make the

Flathead screws can be countersunk so that the top of the head is flush with the surface of the board (left). If the head of the screw is driven in deeper, wood filler will conceal the screw. When the furniture is going to be given a natural finish, wood plugs or wood buttons (right half of sketch) should be used.

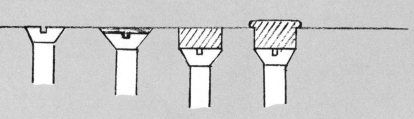

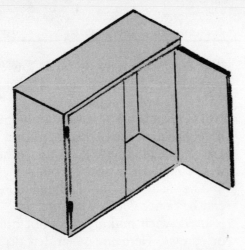

plugs, set the plugs in so that the grain runs in the same direction as the surface or at right angles to it.

4. Another method of concealing the head of the screw is to use wood screw-hole buttons. These are similar to plugs, but they have a rounded or oval top surface and some also have a distinct head. They extend slightly above the surface of the wood and can be obtained in matching or contrasting hardwoods.

How To Hang Swinging Doors

There are many different styles and designs of hinges from which to select when you mount swinging doors on a cabinet. Usually, the better hinges come with mounting instructions, some even with templates or patterns, to make attaching the doors a simple job.

Here are several different ways in which hinges can be added to swinging doors and cabinets.

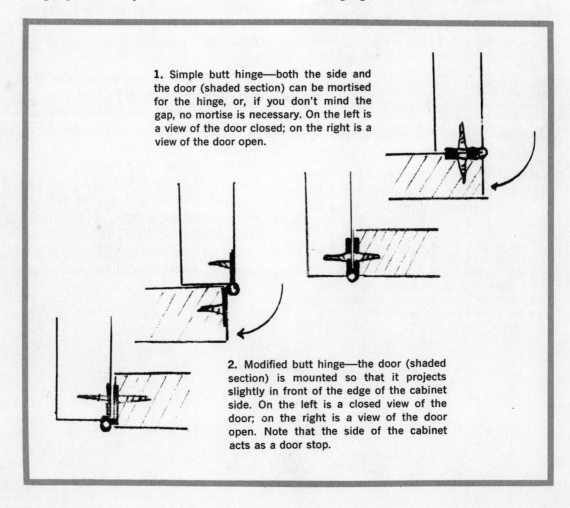

1. Simple butt hinge—both the side and the door (shaded section) can be mortised for the hinge, or, if you don't mind the gap, no mortise is necessary. On the left is a view of the door closed; on the right is a view of the door open.

2. Modified butt hinge—the door (shaded section) is mounted so that it projects slightly in front of the edge of the cabinet side. On the left is a closed view of the door; on the right is a view of the door open. Note that the side of the cabinet acts as a door stop.

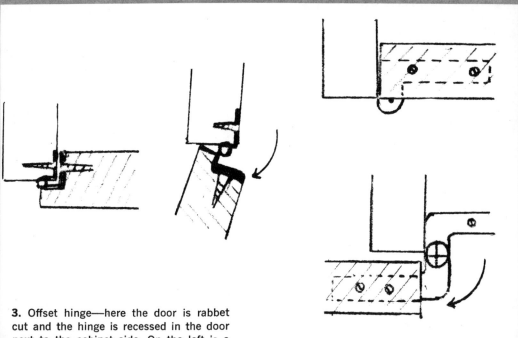

3. Offset hinge—here the door is rabbet cut and the hinge is recessed in the door next to the cabinet side. On the left is a view of the door in the closed position; on the right is a view of the door (shaded section) in the open position. Note that the door does not open all the way.

4. Pivot hinge—the hinge is attached to the top and bottom edge of the door (shaded section) and the top and base of the cabinet. On the left is a view of the door closed; on the right is a view of the door in an open position. With this type of hinge the door opens all the way.

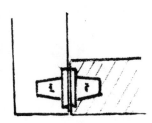

5. Invisible hinge—if you don't want any hinge shown, you can use Soss invisible hinges. They are made in many sizes for different door thicknesses. On the left is a view of the door (shaded section) closed; on the right is a view of the door open all the way.

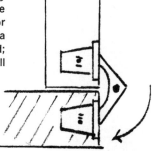

Sketches courtesy of Allen Larkin Associates

How To Make a Desk Top Door

When making furniture, you may want to provide for a writing surface —a desk top—which is not visible when the cabinets are closed. The basic unit is similar to any other type of cabinet construction. The door, instead of being hinged at the side, is hinged at the bottom.

Regular butt hinges or a piano hinge—a continuous hinge strip—is fastened to the cabinet base and the lower section of the door. When the door opens forward and downward, it becomes a desk top. To keep the desk top-door level with the floor, support braces are added as shown in the sketch. These are available in many different styles and are made of steel or solid brass. A support on each side will support the desk top as a writing surface.

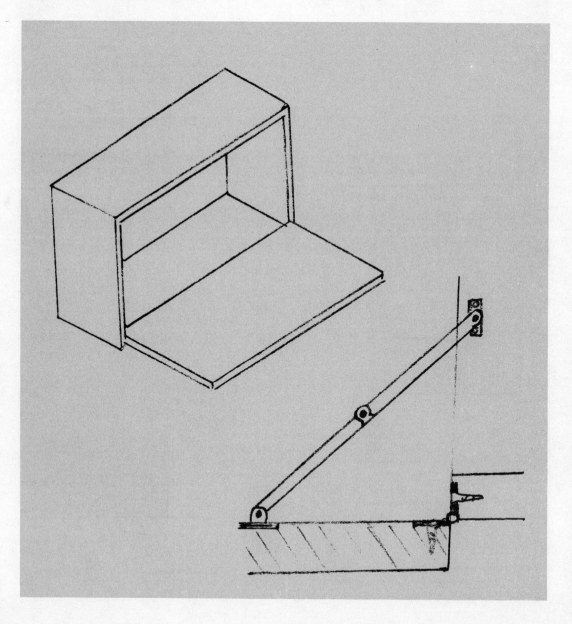

How To Install a Vanity Lift Door

Another type of hinged door is sometimes found when making a vanity unit. The top of a section lifts upward and back and a mirror is attached to the underside of this piece.

Actually, this is a modified hinged door, which when it is opened fully forms an angle of 105° to 115° with the top surface. Construction of the top, sides and base of the unit is along the lines outlined previously in this section. There are, however, two modifications necessary for the proper working of the door.

1. The rear edge of the door (shaded section) is cut at an angle to permit easy opening and closing.

2. The forward edge of the back filler strip (cross hatched section) is cut with a matching angle to permit the door to move freely.

Pivot hinges are best for this installation. The double cut of the rear edge of the door and back filler strip eliminates the need for any door stop. The door opens to the fullest extent and then comes to rest against the filler strip.

While it is possible to use butt hinges or a piano hinge for this installation, some provision must be made to hold the counter top-door combination open at the proper angle. This addition spoils the graceful line of the cabinets.

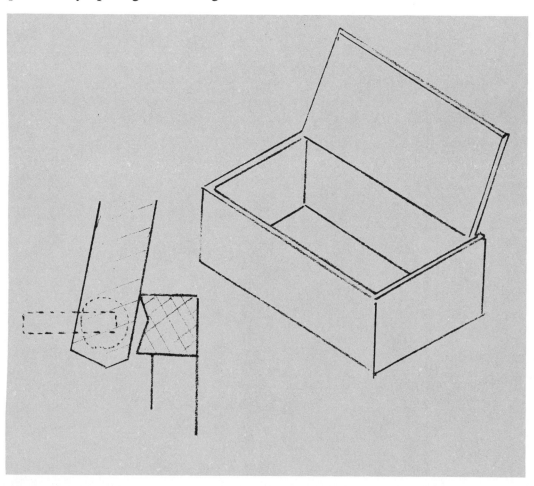

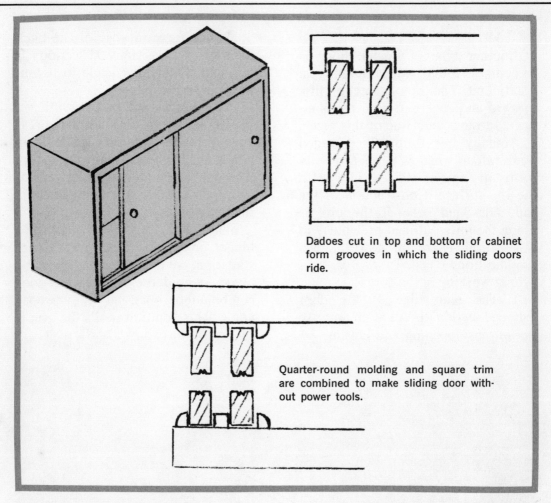

Dadoes cut in top and bottom of cabinet form grooves in which the sliding doors ride.

Quarter-round molding and square trim are combined to make sliding door without power tools.

How To Make Sliding Doors

Sliding doors are very popular in contemporary furniture. The use of this type of door makes it possible to open a cabinet without having the doors swing out where they may get in the way.

Whether you have power tools or not, it is simple to make sliding doors for a cabinet. You have a choice of many materials to use for sliding doors—tempered hardboard, perforated hardboard, plywood, flat reinforced fiber glass, mirror, glass and Novoply. One important point to remember about sliding doors is that you must use a material which will not warp.

How thick the door material should be depends upon the size of the door and the method used to make the doors slide. Normally, ½″ or ¾″ material presents no problem in cabinet doors. However, ⅛″ tempered hardboard or ¼″ plywood may buckle or warp if the door is of any substantial size. Select the material for the door carefully before you start to make the necessary provisions for installation.

Here are several different ways in which you can install sliding doors in cabinets or built-ins. Some require the use of power tools; others need nothing more than simple hand tools.

DADOES WITH FLUSH DOORS
—Two dadoes cut into the bottom surface of the cabinet top and two dadoes in the top surface of the cabinet base provide the grooves in which the doors will slide. Here are several pointers to help you make the proper size cuts:

1. The width of each dado should be equal to the thickness of the sliding door plus $\frac{1}{16}''$ to $\frac{1}{8}''$.

2. The forward edge of the front dado should be about $\frac{1}{2}''$ from the edge of the board, $\frac{1}{4}''$ at the minimum.

3. The space between the two dadoes should be at least $\frac{1}{8}''$ but preferably $\frac{1}{4}''$.

4. The depth of the dado cut into the top of the cabinet should be double the depth of the dado cut in the bottom of the cabinet.

5. The height of the door should be the distance from the top surface of the bottom of the cabinet to the bottom surface of the cabinet top, plus the depth of the top dado.

6. The width of each door should be one half the distance between the two sides of the cabinet plus at least $\frac{1}{4}''$ and a maximum of $\frac{1}{2}''$.

7. When installing the doors, set the rear one in place before the front one.

8. To set a door in place, insert the top into the top dado and then lower it into the bottom dado.

9. To remove a door, lift it all the way up into the top dado and pull the bottom edge forward.

CLEAT METHOD—If you don't have power tools, it is possible to make sliding doors by using pieces of $\frac{1}{4}''$ or $\frac{3}{8}''$ square trim molding as guides. Here is all you have to do

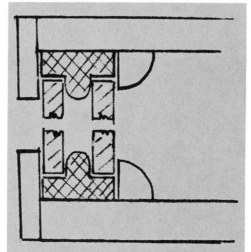

Screen slide molding (cross-hatched section) makes a perfect track for $\frac{1}{8}''$ tempered hardboard or $\frac{1}{4}''$ plywood doors.

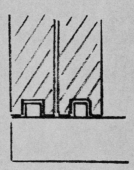

Dadoes or grooves cut into bottom and top edges of doors fit over special square track for easy-to-make sliding doors.

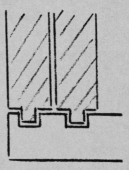

Dadoes cut in underside of cabinet top and top surface of cabinet base provide the tracks in which the doors will ride. Top and bottom edges are cut with a tongue to fit into the dadoes.

(this is based on using ¼" quarter-round molding, ¼" square molding and ⅛" clearance for each door to slide freely):

1. Measure the thickness of the door and double that figure. To it add 1" and measure off this distance from the front edge of the cabinet along the underside of the cabinet top and top surface of the cabinet base.

2. Cut two pieces of ¼" quarter round to proper length to fit between the cabinet sides and nail it so that the back edge is flush with the lines drawn.

3. Measure the height and width of the door and cut to size.

4. Measure ⅜" from the forward edge of the quarter-round and draw a line along the top and bottom.

5. Cut a piece of ¼" square molding the width of the cabinet.

6. Set the rear door in place and nail this ¼" square strip so that the rear edge is flush with the lines drawn in step 4.

7. Cut two more pieces of ¼" quarter-round to the cabinet width.

8. Set the front door in place and position the forward quarter-round so that the front edge is flush with the forward edge of the cabinet. Then nail in place.

SCREEN SLIDE MOLDING METHOD—Here is another way to make sliding doors without power tools. It involves the use of screen slide molding, which is sold in many lumber yards. You can use ¼" plywood or ⅛" or ¼" tempered hardboard with this molding.

1. Cut two pieces of ⅜" or even ½" quarter round to the width of the cabinet. Nail these in place (as

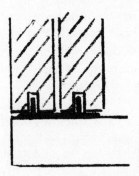

Metal track is used for the doors to slide on. Dadoes or grooves are cut in the top and bottom edges of both doors to ride on the track.

shown in sketch) so that the forward edge is ¾" from the front of the cabinet.

2. Cut two doors to the proper width and height. The height is the distance from the top of the cabinet to the bottom less ⅝".

3. Set the rear door on the screen slide molding (cross-hatched section in sketch) and position the molding so that it is flush against the quarter round already nailed in place.

4. Cut two pieces of trim or decorative molding for the face of the cabinet. They should be equal to the thickness of the top or bottom of the cabinet plus ⅜" or ½".

5. Set front door on screen slide molding and fasten the face trim or decorative molding to the outer edge of the cabinet top and base.

How To Make a Lift and Sliding Door

Another variation in attaching a door is the lift and sliding unit. The door can be mounted in different ways. It can lift up and slide back, drop forward and slide back, or swing forward and slide back. In all three types, the door disappears into the cabinet.

This is a more advanced method of installing a door and is best done with power tools. It is necessary to use pivot hinges and rout out the sides to permit the hinged door to slide back into the cabinet.

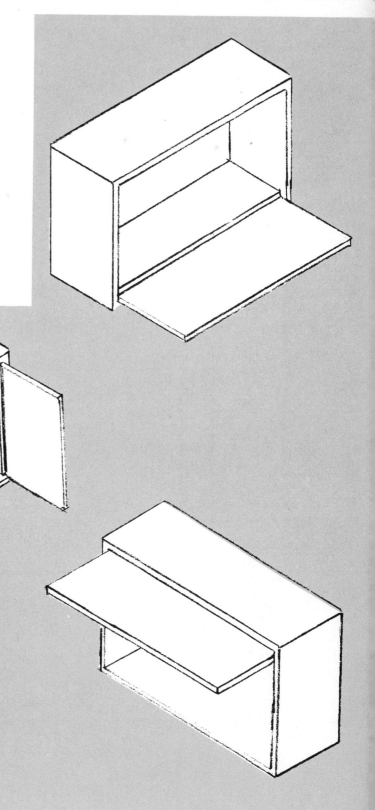

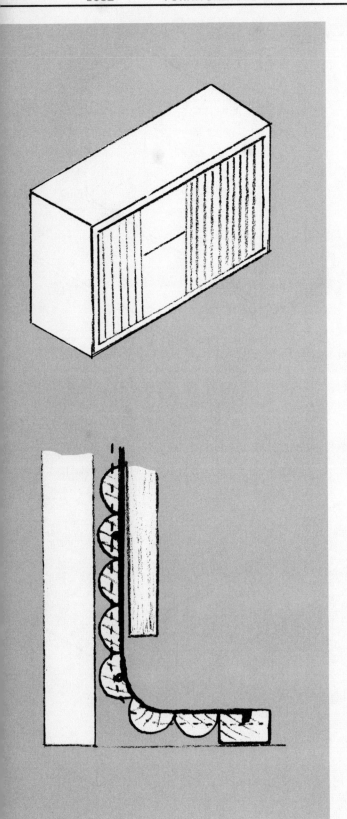

This type of door is particularly useful when a radio is mounted inside the cabinet together with its speaker or when a TV set is installed and you want to get the doors out of the way.

It is necessary, however, to add a false top, bottom or sides, depending upon the way in which the door is hung. The false section (shaded in the sketch) should be equal to the inside depth of the cabinet less the thickness of the door plus ⅛″ to ¼″.

A router will cut the grooves necessary for the pivot hinge to move in when the door is being pushed back into the cabinet. The groove can be cut with a router bit on a drill press or even with an electric drill, but practice a few times with these tools until you have sufficient experience to cut along a straight line and at a constant depth.

How To Make Tambour Doors

Rolling doors that disappear within a cabinet are not difficult to make. They take time but can be built with simple hand tools.

The doors are made by attaching half-round to canvas with adhesive. False sides and back must be added, for the doors will ride between the false side and the cabinet side and then disappear between the false back and cabinet back.

Use a piece of finished molding stock at each end of the door and rabbet cut the rear side to attach the canvas. It is best to use adhesive and tacks to hold the canvas to the molding stock.

A groove must be cut into the underside of the cabinet top and the top surface of the cabinet base for door guides to slide in. The door guides can be finishing nails hammered into the end molding pieces on each door. To keep the door from buckling and to make it ride easily, door guides should be added to every third half round as well.

How To Make Drawers Slide

Nothing is more annoying than a sticky drawer. Therefore, when you make your own furniture or add drawers in a built-in, make provisions for easy-to-slide drawers. Here are several ways in which drawers can be mounted:

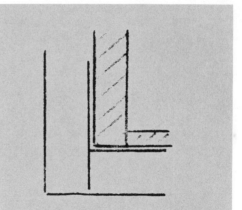

1. The drawer (shaded section) can ride on a board set between the sides of the cabinet. This is the simplest way to do the job but the drawer is not free moving.

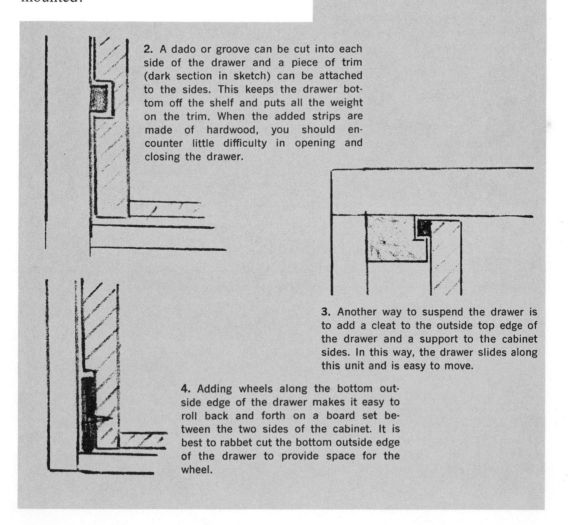

2. A dado or groove can be cut into each side of the drawer and a piece of trim (dark section in sketch) can be attached to the sides. This keeps the drawer bottom off the shelf and puts all the weight on the trim. When the added strips are made of hardwood, you should encounter little difficulty in opening and closing the drawer.

3. Another way to suspend the drawer is to add a cleat to the outside top edge of the drawer and a support to the cabinet sides. In this way, the drawer slides along this unit and is easy to move.

4. Adding wheels along the bottom outside edge of the drawer makes it easy to roll back and forth on a board set between the two sides of the cabinet. It is best to rabbet cut the bottom outside edge of the drawer to provide space for the wheel.

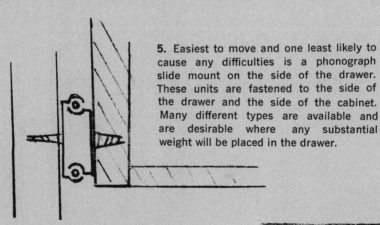

5. Easiest to move and one least likely to cause any difficulties is a phonograph slide mount on the side of the drawer. These units are fastened to the side of the drawer and the side of the cabinet. Many different types are available and are desirable where any substantial weight will be placed in the drawer.

6. This is a modified form of the phonograph slide. Here the unit is mounted on the bottom of the drawer. It is necessary to use two slides for the easiest movement of the drawer. This type of drawer mounting is generally used for phonographs set into cabinets.

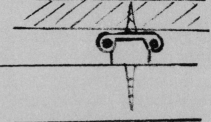

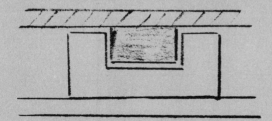

7. A special cleat with a dado cut its full length will act as a drawer guide. A special trim strip is attached to the bottom of the drawer and the cleat to a board set between the cabinet sides. This method can be used with any of the above (except for the phonograph slides) to prevent the drawer from shifting from side to side when being opened and closed.

8. This is a modification of the tongue-and-groove method just described. It is a dovetail slide and serves the same purpose as the one in item 7. It is used primarily by professionals and advanced craftsmen because it requires precise cutting.

The room which appears cluttered with too much furniture, or practically empty without enough of it, may be made more attractive through the optical illusion of color.

Too Large Room

Repaint your furniture if it looks too small and almost lost in the large room. Use a color which is a contrast to the walls. Slipcovers of bright colors should be put on the upholstered furniture. In this manner the furniture will look more important, and will "fill" the room through its eye appeal.

Tiny pictures on the wall of a large room are inappropriate. Put them into larger frames with larger mats; or hang the small pictures in groups to form larger masses on the wall.

Too Small Room

When the furniture appears too heavy and crowds the small room you may create a more spacious feeling by painting the furniture the same color as the walls. The slipcovers and draperies should match and be as near in basic color as the furniture and walls. This gives the illusion of uncluttered space.

If you have large pictures on the wall of a small room, they should be replaced or be cut down; the way

Furniture Camouflage

to do this is to give them narrower mats and smaller frames. Another good idea is to paint the frames the same color as the wall so the pictures won't appear as large as their actual size.

Low Ceilinged Room

The furniture may seem too high for the low room. Why not saw off some of the height of the legs of tables, cabinets, chairs, sofas? This has been done successfully by ingenious homemakers, and the resulting effect is excellent.

An upright piano which seems too tall cannot, of course, be cut down easily. But you can paint it the same color as the wall, and immediately it ceases to be conspicuous. Paint the piano stool or bench the same color, too.

Very tall, narrow bookshelves may be sawed in half, horizontally, and the two sections placed side by side. This will form a low, wide unit of shelves. If there isn't enough wall space to put them beside each other, they could be used separately.

Major furniture repairs can be largely eliminated by making frequent inspections to detect weak spots, wear, and minor scratches or breaks, and taking care of them before they become serious.

Furniture Care

Solid Surfaces

Shallow surface defects—Sand or plane surface to remove shallow

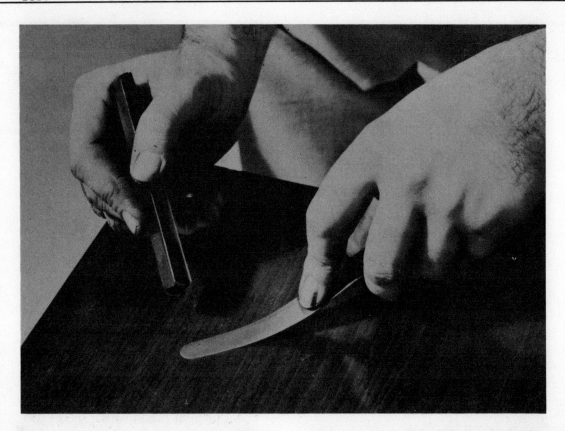

defects in solid wood tops. You can try to fill the dent by raising the wood grain. Place a damp cloth over the dent and set the tip of a medium-hot electric iron on the cloth. The heated water will in many cases cause the dent to vanish.

Deep defects—If a defect is too deep to be removed by sanding or planing, repair it with a shellac stick filler of a matching color. Clean out the scratch, removing all loose or crushed wood fiber. Enlarge it if necessary and undercut slightly. Apply stick shellac with a hot knife blade, filling the depression to surface level. Smooth the fill.

Extensive defects—If the surface is so damaged that neither of the above procedures is practical, cover the entire surface with plywood or tempered hardboard cemented down with woodworking glue or a contact type cement. First, remove the finish and sand the old surface until it is smooth and free of irregularities. Cut edges of the covering flush with the old top edge. If the old edge is marred, use a thin wood banding of the same finish and species as the original surface. Make sure the top edge of the banding is flush with or very slightly under the surface level of the new top. Make the banding wide enough to cover both old edge and surface material. A tempered hardboard surface need not be finished unless it is desired to change the color.

Warped tops—Replace warped tops. To increase stability, use a glued-up board instead of a solid one. For instance, if an 18"x36" top is needed, glue up a top from three 6" pieces, or rip an 18" piece into three 6" pieces turn the center one upside down and reglue.

Veneered Surfaces

Minor defects—Use stick shellac to repair minor defects in veneered surfaces.

Defective areas—If damage is confined to a small area, repair it as follows:

1. Select a patch slightly larger than the damaged section. Apply three or four small spots of glue to the damaged area, press the patch over the glue and allow it to set.

2. With a sharp knife held vertically, cut through both patch and damaged veneer. This cut need not follow a rectangle; it is better to taper it to a point at each end.

3. Detach the patch and clean out the damaged veneer within the cut area. Apply glue, insert patch, and place a weight on it. Remove excess glue from the surface and allow the repair to set.

Locks and Catches

Minor shrinkage or warpage can make door locks and catches fail to work properly. To correct this condition, shift strike plates or adjust hinge positions.

Drawers

Sticking drawers can be freed by sanding or planing sides or bottom. Apply powdered soapstone to relieve minor sticking. A slight readjustment of the drawer guides may eliminate a great deal of work on a warped drawer. If glue joints at corners show signs of loosening, repair them with glue blocks, prefer-

ably triangular or quarter-round in cross section, to prevent dovetail corners from breaking. Do not repair loose corners with brads; they may split the wood and do not equal glue blocks for strength.

Fastenings and Attachments

Enlarged screw and nail holes—Screw or nail holes often become enlarged, with resultant loosening of hinges, strike plates, latches, handles, and similar fittings. Fill such holes with composition wood or a soft wood plug. Replace the fitting and fasten it securely.

Wear around fittings—If wood surfaces around a fitting become seriously worn, remove the fitting, inlay a new piece of wood in the worn area, and refasten the fitting. If this is not practicable, relocate fitting. Use the following method to relocate butt hinges for doors or lids:

1. Mortise door or lid to a depth equal to the double hinge thickness. This eliminates the second mortise and reduces chances of an error in marking or mortising.

2. Fasten hinges on door or lid. Cut off one screw just long enough to project about $\frac{1}{16}$" through the hinge when it is closed and the screw is in place. File a point on this stub and set it in the hinge.

3. Set door or lid in position and press hinge against frame. Drill screw hole in frame at point marked by stub screw. Then fasten hinges to frame.

Miscellaneous Repairs

Splits or cracks—Repair lengthwise splits or cracks extending entirely through a member by forcing

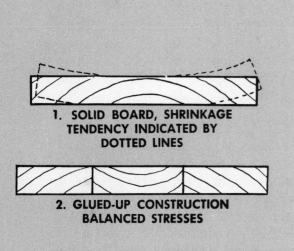

1. SOLID BOARD, SHRINKAGE TENDENCY INDICATED BY DOTTED LINES

2. GLUED-UP CONSTRUCTION BALANCED STRESSES

To prevent shrinkage shown in (1), rip board into thirds, invert center section, and reglue.

glue into crack and then applying pressure to close it. Maintain pressure until glue is dry.

For larger repairs, such as broken legs of chairs and table, refer to *FURNITURE REPAIRS, GLUED*.

Metal

Chairs and tables made with metal frames are sometimes hurt through exposure to dampness or rain (especially outdoor furniture). To correct this condition, first brush all rust off carefully. Wash the metal surface with benzine (caution: flammable!) then apply a coat of protecting paint; a red lead primer is usually preferred. When it is dry, paint a second coat (and a third coat if you desire) of any outdoor paint suitable for metal.

Furniture which is made of chromium plate may show signs of wear and become chipped. It may not be possible to do a good refinishing job at home. It is suggested that the furniture be taken to a metal shop for a professional job of replating.

Leather

To clean leather on furniture, use lukewarm water with mild soap flakes and a teaspoonful of vinegar. Dip a clean, soft cloth into the water, and rub it over the leather. Then go over it with the cloth wrung out in clear lukewarm water, to wash off any suds.

When it is thoroughly dry, polish the leather with a lamb's-wool shoe brush or a dry, soft cloth onto which you have squeezed a dab of neutral leather dressing from a tube. This cream also comes in liquid form in a bottle, and may be obtained at any notion counter or shoe repair shop.

Insects in Furniture

Termites or other insects may enter the furniture; they must be exterminated the moment their presence is discovered. You may buy liquid insect removers in the drug or paint store, and follow manufacturer's directions. Or, you may try to squirt them out with kerosene or gasoline put into a small spray or oil can. (Be very cautious, however, as these fuels are flammable!) You might try hydrogen peroxide for squirting into very small crevices or holes in furniture, and this sometimes helps.

Painting Furniture

For information on methods of painting, varnishing, enameling or otherwise finishing furniture, refer to the section on *FURNITURE FINISHING* and *PAINTING*.

Furniture Finishing

After completing the woodworking phase of furniture making, you are ready to add the finishing touches. A good finish on the furniture will add much to its appearance. No matter how good your workmanship or the quality of the lumber used, a poor finish will result in an unsatisfactory job. Therefore, decide upon the best finish for your particular purpose and apply it carefully.

Likewise, if you are remodeling old furniture, it is necessary to maintain quality workmanship unfinishing. Here you will find information about preparing surfaces for finishing as well as different finishes.

Check List of Finishing Materials

1. Commercial paint and varnish remover
2. Commercial wood bleach
3. Sealers—White shellac, orange shellac, white shellac enamel (for limed effects), clear and white resin sealers, lacquer sealer
4. Stains—Penetrating oil stains, pigmented or wiping oil stains, non-grain-raising stains, colors-in-oil to tint resin sealers
5. Fillers—Paste wood filler, lacquer sanding sealer, spackling compound, wood putty, stick shellac
6. Undercoats—Flat enamel un-

dercoat, exterior primer.
7. Finishing coats — satin, semi-gloss or gloss varnish; brushing or spraying lacquer; enamel, interior or exterior; paste furniture wax
8. Thinners—Turpentine, mineral spirits, alcohol

9. Rubbing materials—Sandpaper, waterproof sandpaper, silicon-carbide paper, steel wool, rubbing compound, pumice stone, rottenstone, rubbing oil
10. Paint brushes
11. Spray equipment
12. Miscellaneous — Clean rags, cheesecloth, painter's duster, rubbing felt, sandpaper block or portable electric sander

Cleaning and Repairing Wood Surfaces

1. Before removing the old finish, repair loose joints, splits, cracks and other blemishes in the furniture. The old finish will give your furniture protection against additional scratches, mars and glue stains during the process of making repairs. Any surface scratches, gouges and abrasions should be resurfaced after the old finish is removed.

2. Apply any good commercial paint and varnish remover to the piece of furniture. Follow the manufacturer's instructions for proper application.

3. To remove the old finish from curved areas, ornamental carvings or spindles use a very fine bristled steel brush or steel wool wrapped around a pointed dowel stick or lollipop stick. Burlap, cut into strips of varying widths, can be used to remove the softened finish from turned pieces. Fine steel wool entwined with cord is effective in removing the softened finish from crevices on rounded surfaces. Steel wool on electrician's or Scotch tape is also useful for removing the finish from rounded surfaces where the see-saw motion will help you to work quickly and efficiently.

4. When the furniture is cleaned of the old finish, scrub the clean, bare surface with #2 steel wool dipped in denatured alcohol. You can also sand with fine sandpaper and wash down with a cloth dampened in gum turpentine. The washing chemical best suited for use will depend upon the type of remover you use. Be sure to follow the manufacturer's instructions for best results.

5. Scars, dents, and mars must be smoothed out for a professional job and smooth surface. Shallow dents can be raised with damp cloth and a hot iron. Deeper mars should be filled with a crack filler or with stick shellac, which comes in many colors, applied hot and spread with a knife blade or palette knife. After the crack filler has hardened, sand smooth with medium fine sandpaper, rubbing with the grain of the wood.

6. Weather stains or dark woods can be bleached to the shade you desire by using a commercial wood bleach, fresh peroxide, or an oxalic acid solution. Wear rubber gloves when working with these solutions. When the surface is dry, wash well with a solution of 50% warm water and 50% white vinegar. Allow the surface to dry thoroughly and sand the entire surface with medium fine sandpaper.

Stain, Shellac and Varnish

1. If you plan to stain or bleach the furniture and finish with shellac or varnish, sandpaper the surface with fine sandpaper. (New unpainted furniture, even if it feels smooth to the touch, should be sanded with fine sandpaper before applying any finish.) Be sure that the grain of the

wood is open so that it will uniformly accept the stain or bleach. Follow the manufacturer's instructions for the use of and neutralization of the bleach. If this process is not done properly, the bleach may affect the subsequent coats of finish and ruin the entire job.

2. After staining or bleaching, you may want to fill the open-grained woods such as oak, mahogany and walnut for a smoother surface. Close-grained woods such as pine, maple and birch do not need filler. Paste filler can be obtained in colors; however, if the color you want is not available, natural filler can be tinted with the stain being used or mixed with colors-in-oil.

3. An easy way to apply the paste filler is to spread the filler vigorously across and with the grain with an old stubby but clean paint brush. Rub it well into the grain. When the filler loses its gloss, rub away the excess across the grain with a pad formed of coarse burlap.

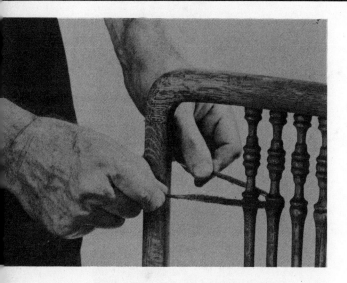

4. After the filler has dried thoroughly, the surface should be smoothed carefully with #3/0 sandpaper. Remember that you cannot obtain a professional finish unless you prepare the surface properly. Sanding the furniture surface as smoothly as possible is most important. Always dust and wipe the furniture you are working on to keep it dry and dust free.

5. The exposed end grain of wood in furniture is as absorbent as a sponge and it will soak up too much stain unless properly sealed or unless you prefer this contrast. Seal this end grain with a thin coat of clear shellac before the stain is applied. Be careful not to permit the shellac to flow onto the side grain. If it does, sand off completely before applying stain; otherwise an uneven finish will result.

6. Allow the stain to dry for 24 hours. If necessary, stain again and wipe again according to instructions until you have produced the desired shade. Let the final coat of stain dry for 24 hours. Seal the stain with a coat of white shellac. Thin your shellac 50-50 with denatured alcohol and flow on with a brush. Be sure to brush with the grain. Don't go back over the wet shellacked areas. If a spot is skipped, touch it up later when the coat is dry.

7. When the shellac is dry—allow at least three hours—smooth carefully and lightly with #3/0 steel wool.

8. Finish the furniture with two or three coats of clear satin-finish varnish.

9. Flow on the varnish carefully, brushing with the grain. Don't try to brush back over it. Watch for runs and smooth them out carefully before they have an opportunity to set.

10. Between the application of each coat and after the final coat, rub carefully and lightly with #3/0 steel wool. Dust with a rag soaked in turpentine.

11. Protect the final coat of varnish with an application of good furniture wax.

12. Do your finishing work in a dust free, well-ventilated, dry room.

Lacquer Finish

To lacquer a piece of furniture the old finish must be removed down to the bare wood. You cannot apply lacquer over paint, enamel or varnish. Follow the steps 1 through 5 described in "Cleaning and Preparing Wood Surfaces."

If you are using clear lacquer, apply stain to the wood to arrive at the desired finish. Follow steps 1 through 6 under "Stain, Shellac and Varnish." But eliminate any shellac or varnish steps.

Lacquer should be applied in a dust-free room, at a temperature of at least 70°F. Set up a fan in the room and avoid any fire or flame near the work. If you intend to apply the lacquer with a brush, be sure to get brushing lacquer. Spraying lacquer dries too quickly to spread with a brush.

1. The first coat is the primer. Both the primer and lacquer should be thinned to a milk-thick consistency. Primer as well as lacquer itself should be flowed on with a single stroke and permitted to level itself. Use the best soft varnish brush that you can buy for professional results and really fine craftsmanship.

2. When the primer is dry, smooth it with fine waterproof sandpaper dipped in water to remove the fine specks. Dry the furniture with an absorbent lint-free cloth.

3. Apply the lacquer as it comes from the can if you intend to use only one coat. For two or more coats, and a much tougher surface, thin the lacquer with one third its amount of thinner.

4. Between coats, sand carefully and lightly with fine sandpaper used wet.

5. Give the final coat a rich velvety sheen by rubbing down with a commercial rubbing compound or rottenstone.

REMOVING SCARS ON LACQUERED SURFACES—After the lacquer has hardened, a sharp blow on the surface may leave a white scar. To remove the scar:

1. Place a drop of lacquer thinner on the surface by using a tooth-

Small holes, gouges, deep scratches and cracks can be patched with stick shellac. These sticks are available in matching wood colors and are best applied by heating a putty knife to melt some of the shellac and force it into the dent in the surface.

A moderately-hot electric iron and a damp cloth will raise and even out dents in many wood surfaces. This process can be used on a finished surface but you must exercise care not to scorch the finish with the iron.

pick, matchstick or dropper.

2. Don't touch the surface or the scar itself with the tool used to apply the lacquer thinner.

3. The thinner will soften the lacquer surface enough to remove the whitish appearance of the scar. After the lacquer thinner evaporates the lacquer will harden and the surface will be restored to its original appearance.

Enamel Finish

The durable, washable surface of enamel is due to its varnish base. However, the hardness makes it brittle and liable to chip or flake unless a careful job of preparation and application is performed. To enamel furniture surfaces:

1. Follow the steps outlined for cleaning and preparing the surface described earlier in the text.

2. Seal the wood with a wash coat of shellac (50% shellac-50% denatured alcohol). The shellac will help prevent the grain from showing through the enamel.

3. After the shellac is dry, smooth lightly with #3/0 steel wool. Sandpaper doesn't work too well because shellac has a tendency to clog.

Old paint, varnish and lacquer can be removed by using a paint remover. After the liquid is applied, let the work stand for several minutes until the surface bubbles. Then remove the old finish with a putty knife. It is best to work in a well-ventilated place and to use a non-inflammable paint remover.

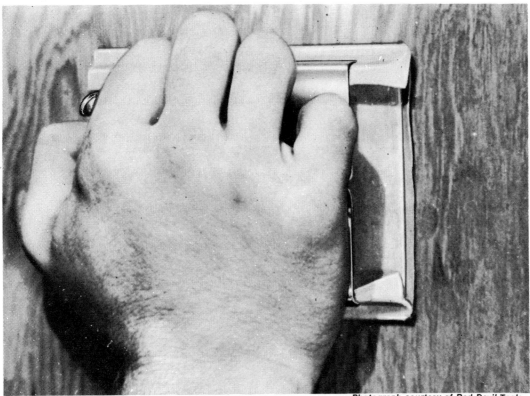

Photograph courtesy of Red Devil Tools.

Sand all surfaces before finishing. Always sand with the grain using a sanding block when working by hand or an electric sander for big surfaces.

4. Tint the enamel undercoat if you plan a single finishing coat of dark enamel. Mix ¾ of the undercoat with ¼ of the enamel to be used. Enamel undercoat needs a thorough stirring. Pour off the top liquid, stir the pigment until it is smooth, return the liquid slowly as you stir it in.

5. Apply the undercoat and brush it out thoroughly. Avoid a heavy, gummy undercoat. Don't overload your brush. Start painting at a top piece on the furniture and work down. Watch carefully for sags and runs, brush them out before they harden.

6. Smooth the undercoat with #3/0 sandpaper after you have permitted the surface to dry for at least 24 hours. Use a light touch on the undercoat because it is a soft surface and easy to cut through into the wood. Dust with a turpentine-soaked rag.

7. If two or more colors are to be used, apply masking tape to stop the finishing coats on a straight line and to prevent running. Brush on the finish and strip off the tape *before* the finish hardens. Flow on enamel in small squares and smooth with a very light cross brushing. Dip in only half of the brush to avoid overloading with enamel. Work rapidly and don't overbrush.

8. One coat usually will cover; two will add durability. Roughen the first coat slightly with fine sandpaper

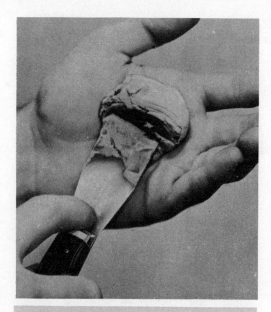

Putty or wood filler should be used to fill all holes left by countersunk screws or counterset nails. Force the material into the hole, leaving a slight amount protruding. Most fillers shrink as they dry; you can sand off the excess.

after it dries and before you apply the second coat. A good wax can be applied if desired, for added protection.

Oil Polish Finish

To get a beautiful rich finish on hardwoods:

1. Brush boiled linseed oil on raw smoothly sanded furniture and let it soak in, then polish long and vigorously with a soft cloth.

2. Repeat each week until you have reached the desired color and sheen. Let dry for a few days.

3. Apply a thin coat of shellac and two coats of wax.

Charred Finish

A surface charring and hardening with flame presents an interesting and easy finish for the handyman to apply to new or old furniture. Two pieces of equipment—a torch and a stiff bristle brush—are all that are needed for the project. Practice on an old plank or board first. The following steps outline the char finish:

1. The furniture to be finished must be dry and free from any paint or inflammable material.

2. Light the torch, adjust the flame and pass the flame from the torch back and forth in smooth sweeps over the surface of the wood. This will produce an even over-all char on the surface of the wood. Be careful not to burn too deeply.

3. Inside joints and corners require a bit more care. Watch for a circle of yellow flame which indicates that you're beginning to burn too deep. Don't try to burn joint lines too deep and dark or try to match the adjacent surfaces. Brushing later will darken and even off this area.

4. After the charring operation, comes brushing. Use a stiff bristle brush to brush out the soft char. Brush lightly with the grain and blow the dust away as you work. Brush in the corners with a toothbrush or similar small brush. Brush and char alternately until you have produced the desired shade and grain effect.

5. Shellac or varnish the surface to protect the finish. Paste wax can also be used to seal the surface and repeated waxings will produce a whitish flecked surface which resembles an old worn and antique finish.

Plain Sliced Oak Pickled Stain

1. Natural   paste   wood   filler

thinned according to directions with turpentine or mineral spirits; to this mix add 15% white Firzite.

2. Apply as per directions, being sure to rub well into pores and off the surface completely. Let dry 24 hours.

3. Two or three coats Satinlac; each coat steel wooled with #3/0 steel wool, left dull.

Philippine Mahogany, Light Finish

1. Natural paste wood filler tinted with approximately 2 level teaspoons each burnt sienna and burnt umber in oil to 1 quart of thinned natural filler.

2. Apply as per instructions. Let dry 24 hours.

3. Two or three coats Satinlac; each coat steel-wooled, left dull.

Birch Blond Finish

1. White Firzite thinned 20% as per direction.

2. Apply, let penetrate about 5 minutes, rub well into wood and clean off. Let dry 24 hours.

3. Two or three coats Satinlac; each coat steel-wooled, left dull.

Honduras Mahogany Light Medium Finish

1. Stain with a mixture of 3 parts Adam and 1 part Sheraton Satin-stain and 6 parts water. Let dry overnight. Sandpaper with #3 or 4/0 paper without cutting through and be sure to dust out pores.

2. Fill with natural paste wood filler tinted with 2 teaspoonsful of burnt sienna and 2 of burnt umber in oil to one quart of thinned natural filler. Apply as per directions.

3. Two or three coats Satinlac; each coat steel-wooled with #3/0 steel wool, left dull.

Walnut, Medium Warm Finish

1. Fill with natural filler tinted with 2 teaspoonsful umber, 2 teaspoonsful burnt sienna to one quart natural filler thinned.

2. Apply as per directions, being sure to rub well into pores and off the surface. Let dry 24 hours.

3. Two or three coats Satinlac; each coat steel-wooled with #3/0 steel wool, left dull.

Honey Color Maple Finish

1. Stain with weak walnut alcohol or water stain.

2. Dry 1½ hours.

A blowtorch is useful when removal of paint is necessary. However, you should exercise care to avoid starting a fire or burning the surface. As the paint softens, scrape off using a flexible putty knife.

Photograph courtesy of Red Devil Tools.

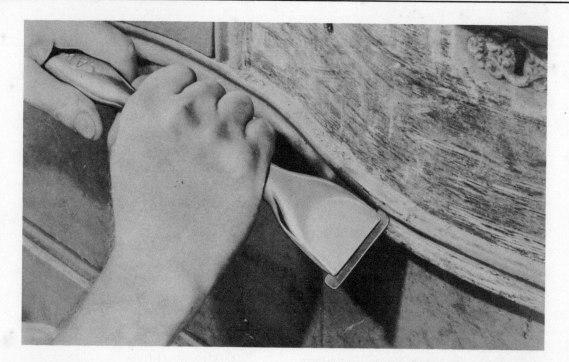

3. Scuff with medium sandpaper.

4. Flow on thinned shellac with brush.

5. Dry four hours.

6. Cover with another coat of thinned shellac.

7. Dry overnight.

8. Rub with medium waterproof sandpaper. Lubricate with 8 parts Savasol #5 and 1 light rubbing oil or thin mineral spirits.

9. Rub with sandpaper, lubricate again as in step 8.

10. Wax with good paste wax, let dry 20 minutes and buff.

Light Modern Maple Finish

1. Bleach with aspen concentrate decolorant or wood bleach.

2. Dry 1½ hours.

3. Scuff with medium sandpaper.

4. Flow on thinned shellac with brush.

5. Dry four hours and coat again with shellac.

6. Dry overnight and lubricate as described in step 8, "Honey Color Maple Finish."

7. Sand and repeat lubricating process.

8. Wax, dry 20 minutes, buff.

Faded Mahogany Finish

1. Bleach with weak solution of Behlen Decolorant.

2. Dry overnight.

3. Fill with walnut filler and rub off excess across grain.

4. Scuff with medium sandpaper.

5. Brush on thinned shellac. Dry four hours.

6. Steel-wool with #3/0 steel wool.

7. Brush on another coat of thinned shellac. Dry overnight.

8. Steel-wool again. Wax, let dry 20 minutes, buff.

Natural Oak Finish

1. Scuff with medium sandpaper.

2. Flow on thinned shellac with brush. Let dry four hours.

3. Scuff again as in step one. Coat with thinned shellac and dry overnight.

4. Rub with medium waterproof sandpaper, lubricate with mixture 8 parts Savasol No. 5 and 1 part light rubbing oil or thin mineral spirits.

5. Wax with good paste wax, let dry and buff.

Gray Birch Finish

1. Brush stain mixture, ½ teaspoon No. 8 Behlen's to ½ gallon water, add small amount of No. 96 orange. Dry for four hours.

2. Brush on thinned coat of shellac. Let dry for four hours.

3. Scuff with medium sandpaper, coat with shellac and dry overnight.

4. Rub with waterproof sandpaper, lubricate with mixture 8 parts Savasol No. 5 and 1 part light rubbing oil. Rub again with fine waterproof sandpaper and lubricate again as in step 4, "Natural Oak Finish." Wax and polish.

Ebonized Mahogany Finish

1. Stain furniture with water stain mixture of 8 tablespoons of No. 8 Behlen to ½ gallon of water. Dry 1½ hours.

2. Scuff with medium sandpaper. Brush on coat of thinned shellac and let dry for four hours.

3. Steel-wool with #3/0 and flow on another coat of thinned shellac. Dry overnight. Steel-wool again.

4. Wax with good paste wax, dry and buff.

Bleached Pickled Pine Finish

1. Bleach with solution aspen

White vinegar and warm water are sometimes used to clean wood surfaces after they have been bleached with a commercial bleach or peroxide. After this application is finished, let the wood dry and then sand.

It is usually necessary to sand all surfaces lightly between the various finishing coats. Use a fine sandpaper and work
with the grain.
Photograph courtesy of Monsanto Chemical Co.

concentrate decolorant or any good
commercial bleach. Dry overnight
and scuff with medium sandpaper.

2. Pickle with thinned solution of
white shellac enamel. Dry overnight.
Coat with thinned white shellac and
denatured alcohol. Dry four hours.
Cover again with another application
of thinned shellac. Dry overnight.

3. Steel-wool with #3/0. Wax with
paste wax, dry and buff.

Natural Korina Finish

1. Sand smooth to touch with fine
sandpaper. Dust.

2. Apply red or brown mahogany
alcohol or water stain to shade desired, according to manufacturer's
instructions. Dry overnight.

3. Brush on thinned solution of
shellac and denatured alcohol. Allow
to dry for three hours.

4. Steel-wool lightly and dust. Apply a second coat of shellac and dry
overnight.

5. With a fine Wet-or-Dry sandpaper, lubricated with light machine
oil, rub with the grain. Wax and allow to dry for 20 minutes; buff to
high luster.

Knotty Pine Finish

1. Sand surfaces smooth to touch
with fine sandpaper. Dust.

2. Apply very light pine or oak
water or alcohol stain to depth of
color desired and according to manufacturer's directions. Dry overnight.
Flow on thinned shellac. Do not go
over wet shellacked areas. Allow the
first coat to dry three hours.

3. Steel-wool lightly with #3/0
and dust.

4. Apply second coat thinned
shellac and dry overnight.

5. Rub with fine Wet-or-Dry sandpaper and machine oil, with the grain.
For a smooth luster, wax, let dry for
20 minutes and buff.

Repair Mahogany Scratches

1. Clean area of wax, oil or polish
with rag dampened in gum turpentine.

2. If the scratch is down into
white wood and the furniture is red
mahogany, stain with household io-
dine. When dry, polish with dark
wax.

3. If the scratch is too big and
deep, use a shellac stick of the same
shade to fill the scar. Let dry and
sand smooth with fine sandpaper.
Polish with wax.

Also see *ANTIQUING,
BLEACHING* and *BLONDE FIN-
ISHING.*

HOW TO FINISH DOUGLAS FIR PLYWOOD

It's easy to get professional-looking results with clean, smoothly sanded Douglas fir plywood. But remember, for best results use only top-quality materials and follow these few simple rules.

Plywood takes paint well — but that doesn't mean it can be applied carelessly. The quality of the finish depends upon the care with which it is applied. Be sure to prepare the surface properly; you can't do a good job if you are painting over dirt and dust or grease. Fill nail holes and wood blemishes in the face or edge of panels with putty or spackle, then sand smooth.

If you want attractive, durable finishes, you'll find top-quality paints, varnishes and stains are the most economical in the long run. Some products require primer coats of compatible formulations. Your local paint dealer will help you choose the right product for the job you have in mind. Read manufacturers' directions carefully; follow them for best results.

Natural Finishes

One of the most popular finishes for Douglas fir plywood wall and ceiling paneling, built-in, cabinets and furniture is the new light stain glaze—a "natural" finish, which retains all the rich, good looks of the natural wood, yet gives contrast in the grain pattern to create warm, colorful effects.

A four-step system is recommended for the finest finish, although satisfactory results are easily obtained following the simple one- or two-step systems.

Apply the finish with a quality brush, starting at the top on vertical surfaces and work downward. Apply liberally, smoothing as you proceed to avoid any heavy concentration and eventual darkening on individual areas.

A limitless variety of interesting colors and shades, ranging from the soft mellow browns and yellows to strong, vivid blues and greens can be obtained by varying the color coat in the instructions to be given.

Remember, when using this or any other natural finish, you'll get a better-looking job if you select plywood panels beforehand with a mind toward appearance and uniform grain pattern.

New Light Stain Glaze

1. *To Whiten Panel*—A coat of interior white undercoat thinned 1 part undercoat to 1 part turpentine or mineral spirits. Before paint film becomes "tacky" (10-15 minutes)

Always remove all traces of wood particles and dust after sanding. Use a clean, dry brush. You don't want any lint left behind to interfere with the flow of your finishing material and leave imperfections on the surface when it has dried. If you don't have a brush handy, use a clean, lint-free cloth.

wipe with a rag or dry-brush so more grain will show through. When dry, sand slightly with fine sandpaper.

2. *To Seal Wood*—One coat of thinned white shellac or clear resin sealer (this seal coat may be thinned more or omitted if greater color penetration is desired). Sand lightly with fine sandpaper when dry.

3. *To Provide Color*—One color coat. This may be interior undercoat or enamel, thinned as for Step No. 1, or color in blending oils. Light stains might also be used. Apply thinly and

wipe or dry-brush to proper color tone. When dry, sand lightly with fine sandpaper.

4. *For Wearing Surface* — One coat of flat varnish. For best effect the varnish may be steel-wooled when dry. A limitless variety of colors and shades may be obtained by changing the color coat.

Economical Finishes

An inexpensive but pleasant blonde finish can be obtained with an easy two-step procedure. First, a coat of interior white undercoat thinned so the wood pattern shows through; the undercoat may be tinted if color is desired. Then, a coat of clear shellac, lacquer or flat varnish.

When using conventional dark stain on fir plywood, first apply clear resin sealer, followed by successive coats of stain and varnish. Sealer may be omitted if greater color contrast is desired.

Paint Finishes

Conventional wall and woodwork paints and enamels are easy to use on Douglas fir plywood. Here again, it pays to use top quality materials. Follow carefully directions on the label regarding mixing, thinning and drying time for each coat.

Interesting textured effects can be obtained with strippling paints—either flat or gloss. This type of finish is easy to apply and covers minor imperfections. For cabinet doors or other surfaces which require cleaning, use washable paints or enamels.

Here are the basic steps to follow in painting or enameling plywood.

1. Fill open surface areas with wood putty. Sand lightly and dust

clean. For additional smoothness, panel edges can be coated with surfacing putty or wood putty. Apply a thin layer and sand smooth when dry.

2. Brush on a flat paint or enamel undercoat. Cover sides and edges. If you discover any unfilled surface blemishes, fill with spackle when coat is dry. Sand lightly and dust clean.

3. Apply second coat of undercoat. For high-gloss enamel finish use undercoat mixed of equal parts flat undercoat and high-gloss enamel. For semi-gloss or flat finish, use undercoat tinted to approximate shade of finish coat. Sand lightly when dry.

4. Apply final coat as it comes from can. This coat as well as preceding coats may be thinned slightly with turpentine or thinner to get better brushability.

A two-coat system consisting of prime and finish coats may also be used.

Stippled Finishes: Textured surfaces may be obtained by priming, followed by a heavy coat of stippling paint. The paint coat may then be textured with a stipple brush, roller or sponge.

Water-thinned Paints: Before applying water-thinned paints, plywood should first be sealed with a clear resin sealer, shellac or flat white paint to prevent grain raise. The paint is

6 STEPS TO INTERIOR FURNITURE FINISHING

1. When you buy a piece of unfinished furniture and want to "do-it-yourself," you will find finishing easy, interesting and rewarding if you follow a few basic rules.

The first thing to do is to sandpaper the surface well. It isn't a long, hard job, but it is important. Before the first coat and between subsequent coats of any material you select, sanding is necessary. You won't get the finish you want without it. Don't let the smooth "feel" of the wood mislead you—almost invisible wood fibers need smoothing out, and dust that settles and dries on the surface between coats must go.

The first sanding, and sanding between applications (except before the final coat) may be done with fine sandpaper. The last sanding should be done with paper of very fine grit. Here the first sanding is being done. The holder for the sandpaper makes your job easier. As the paper becomes worn, a new piece can be slipped into place easily.

2. To remove the traces of wood particles and dust after sanding, a clean, dry brush is best. You don't want any lint left behind to interfere with the flow of your finshing material and to leave imperfections on the surface when it has dried. A clean cloth may be used instead of the brush, but be sure it is lint-free.

then applied according to manufacturer's directions for a sealed surface. If slight grain raise is not objectionable, seal coat may be omitted.

Exterior Finishes

For uses where exposed to weather or moisture, the best paint for regular wood is also best for exterior plywood. High-grade exterior house paints of either TLZ formulation or white-lead-and-oil give excellent service. Avoid paints which set to a hard brittle film.

Edge Sealing: Before installing plywood, seal all edges with a heavy application of high-grade exterior primer, exterior aluminum paint or heavy lead-and-oil paint. In unusually damp localities prime the back of panels before construction starts with a coat of exterior paint.

Painting Procedure—The following three-coat system provides the best results:

1. The primer coat is most important. This coat seals wood, provides a base for following coats. A high-grade exterior primer, thinned with 1 pt. of pure raw linseed oil per gal. of paint or as directed on label, applied with a brush, is recommended. Top quality exterior aluminum house paint also makes a good primer.

2 and 3. Over the prime coat apply second and third coats according to directions on the can.

Other Finishes—Top quality 2-coat TLZ house paints can also be used. However, each coat must be proportionately heavier so that the same dry film thickness as the 3-step system is built up. First brush on primer, thinned as in Step 1 before; then apply second coat according to directions on label.

Textured finishes which have oil or synthetic resin bases are also satisfactory.

Stains, when applied to plywood permanently exposed to the weather, do not provide an adequate protective film for the wood; therefore checking may be expected. Natural finishes usually require extra maintenance.

3. Now you are ready for the first coat. Here, a clear sealer and primer is being used. It doesn't change the color of the wood, but seals the pores to protect the wood against damage by moisture. It also equalizes the hard and soft areas of the wood and makes the subsequent color coat go on evenly. For this reason, stains will not distort the natural beauty of the grain; and paint, if you should decide on that type of finish, will go farther and flow on more smoothly.

The clear sealer and primer, as well as blonding or color-tones in this line of products, is a resin. It does not thicken or become sticky in the can and can be applied very easily and quickly. The clear coat is allowed to "set up" for 15 minutes; then any excess is simply wiped away with a clean cloth. Several hours should be allowed for complete drying.

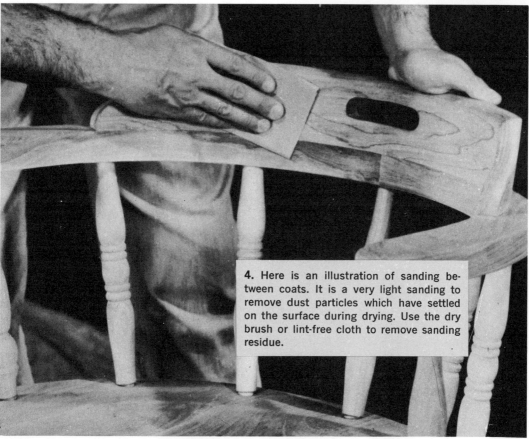

4. Here is an illustration of sanding between coats. It is a very light sanding to remove dust particles which have settled on the surface during drying. Use the dry brush or lint-free cloth to remove sanding residue.

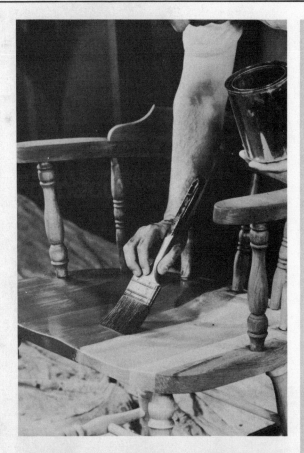

5. There are a number of basic mixes or easy intermixes which give traditional finishes of mahogany, cedar, maple or walnut on the popular-priced woods in much of the unfinished furniture; also, colors of nature found in driftwood, sage, redwood, adobe, etc. The blonding effect, a favorite nowadays, may be achieved by wiping on a white resin sealer; or frosty pastels result from mixing colors-in-oil with the white resin.

Application is the same as for the first clear coat. Simply mix the material well and brush it in to the desired depth of color. This coat is not wiped after a 15-minute "set up." It is brushed on till you attain the effect you want. If a little runs down on a portion of the wood you haven't reached, it will blend in when you get there.

6. After the color coat, you will have sanded lightly again—this time with very fine sandpaper because the next coat is the last one. It's called Satinwood because the wood will look like satin when you are through. It will have a low-luster, hand-rubbed appearance—but no hand-rubbing will be necessary. The Satinwood finish is resistant to alcohol and heat, making counter portion usable, within reason, without fear of damage.

Photograph courtesy of Monsanto Chemical Co.

HOW TO FINISH EXTERIOR FURNITURE

1. Attractive garden furniture adds immensely to the pleasure of outdoor living. But to retain its beauty, wood subjected to hard use and the elements requires extra protection. Color-toning with resin sealers is an effective solution to the problem, and home finishing with products of this type is easy on any wood. The first step is sanding. If you want a professional-type finish, never overlook this step. Almost invisible wood fibers, even on new, unfinished furniture, must be smoothed away. Here a picnic table is being sanded with the aid of a handy holder for the sandpaper. For this step a fine sandpaper is recommended.

2. Wood dust should be completely removed. A clean, dry brush, as shown here, will do the job without leaving lint. If a cloth is used, be sure it is lint-free.

3. Two coats of color-toned resin sealer give a beautiful and durable finish to woods destined for outdoor use. Its careful formulation provides protection against warping, swelling and checking. Pores of the wood are sealed against damaging moisture, and special pigments filter out sun's rays. Color-tones of nature's choice —driftwood, redwood, sage, cedar, mahogany and others achieved by intermixing—blend furniture pleasingly into a garden setting. Resin sealers are not an opaque cover; natural wood grains show through with enhanced beauty. Here a cedar resin stain is being brushed on. Application is easy; the resin does not thicken or become sticky in the can—it "flows" on. Light sanding with very fine sandpaper between first and second coats is recommended.

Furniture Finishing —Adding New Surfaces

In addition to either painting or staining a piece of furniture, it is possible to apply a new surface. This can be a plastic laminate, flexible vinyl plastic or a transfer decal.

The plastic laminate — Formica, Micarta or Consoweld, to name but a few—is cemented to the surface of the wood. It provides a durable surface in wood textures, marble, patterns or decorator colors. It can take substantial punishment and is easy to keep clean. It is, however, moderately expensive when used over large surfaces.

Vinyl plastic, generally used instead of fabric upholstery, can also be used over wood surfaces. It is scuff-resistant and easily kept clean. The vinyl is available in many different gages or thicknesses and comes in many colors and patterns. It is easy to handle for a pair of scissors is all that's needed for cutting.

The transfer decals open new furniture possibilities. Poor woods can be covered with wood-grained or marble sheets. An inexpensive piece of unpainted furniture or a piece you make can be given a rich, new look with this material.

Finishing with Plastic Laminates

This semi-rigid melamine surface comes in sheets as well as rolls and is glued to the wood surfaces with special adhesive. It can be used on new or old furniture.

See sections on *COUNTER TOPS* and *ADHESIVES*.

1. Remove the old finish, using sandpaper and steel wool. Here only the table top is to be finished with melamine plastic laminate.

2. Measure the plastic sheet so that it fits the top of the table with about 1/8" to 1/4" excess around all the edges. Cut to shape with a saw; a coping saw will do.

3. Apply the contact cement with a special notched trowel. Spread the adhesive evenly over the entire top surface.

4. Apply a coat of adhesive to the underside of the plastic surface. When the adhesive dries sufficiently (follow the instructions on the can), set the plastic top in place so that the overlap extends on all four sides.

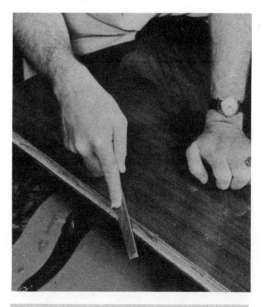

5. Press the plastic surface onto the table top. You can apply the necessary pressure if you borrow your wife's rolling pin.

Photograph courtesy of The Formica Co.

6. Remove the excess around all four edges by filing at an angle until the plastic surface is flush with the edge of the wood. Exert pressure on the down stroke only.

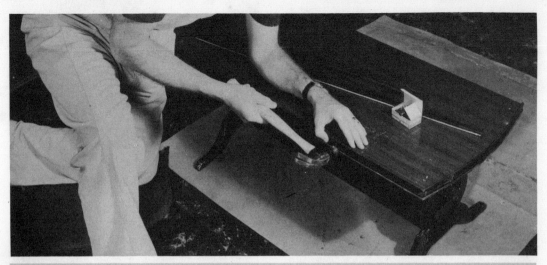

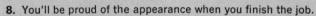

7. You can paint the edge or apply a hardwood trim to conceal the joint between the plastic and the wood.

8. You'll be proud of the appearance when you finish the job.

COVERING A TABLE TOP WITH VINYL PLASTIC

1. Wonders can be performed on a battered-looking old card table right in your own home. All it takes are a few yards of a vinyl plastic upholstery material such as Boltaflex and a hammer and tacks. First, cut the vinyl plastic to fit the table top with an allowance for folding over and under the sides. With the table bottom up and centered over the cut material, tack to the bottom, starting in the center of one side and gradually working out to the corners.

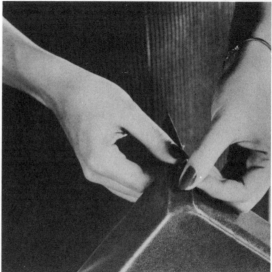

2. As the remaining sides are tacked, stretch the material slightly to keep it smooth and taut. Space tacks about an inch apart and drive them in straight without sinking the tack heads into the vinyl plastic. After all four sides are securely tacked in place, turn the table upright. To make smooth appearing corners, pull each fold gently but firmly to the underside of the table and tack.

3. To finish the table, draw a chalk-line guide around each side. Mark off in two-inch spaces and trim with decorative upholstery tacks.

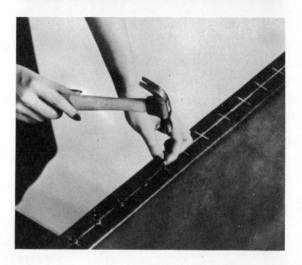

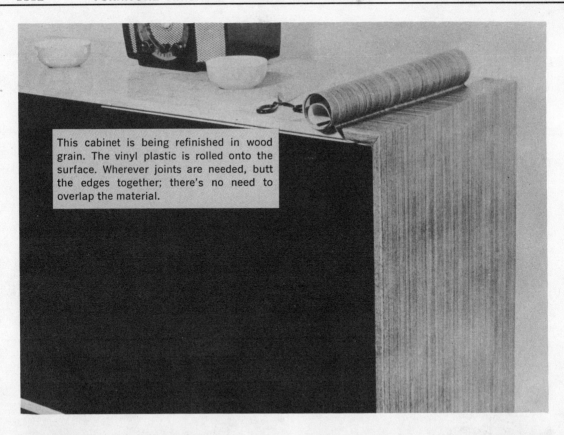

This cabinet is being refinished in wood grain. The vinyl plastic is rolled onto the surface. Wherever joints are needed, butt the edges together; there's no need to overlap the material.

The drawer fronts of this cabinet are being finished to match the wall covering in this room. Note that the self-adhesive vinyl is easy to set even on vertical surfaces.

Photograph courtesy of Monsanto Chemical Co.